The New Fiction

University of Illinois Press   *Urbana Chicago London*

Joe David Bellamy

THE NEW FICTION

Interviews with Innovative

American Writers

LIBRARY OF CONGRESS CATALOGING IN PUBLICATION DATA

Bellamy, Joe David.
   The new fiction.

   1. Authors, American—20th century—Interviews.
2. Fiction. I. Title.
PS135.B4   813'.03   74-14841
ISBN 0-252-00430-2

THIS BOOK IS FOR CONNIE, LAEL, AND SAM BELLAMY

Contents

Preface

Looking back over the last ten years of American fiction writing, one notes that a massive, bewildering change in the literary climate appears to have gathered in energy. Whether the new fiction of the last decade represents a "breakthrough" into fruitful new vistas or the "exhaustion" of a decadent, spent art form, it is, at least, drastically different from the fiction written immediately before by the great American modernists (as they have come to be called) and is based apparently upon totally revised assumptions about the nature and purpose of art. At this point the new fiction is also virtually unassessed and frequently misunderstood. Concurrent with the outpouring of some remarkably innovative fiction during this period, of course, numbers of writers continued to work skillfully in traditional modes, relying basically on nineteenth-century conventions or, in some cases, adapting such conventions for journalistic—or other nonfictional—purposes. In other words, amazing, sweeping, and unanticipated as its appearance has proven to be, the new American fiction is by no means monolithic, ubiquitous, or the result of any conspiracy, though it is no less amazing for that.

In his mid-sixties essay "The Curious Death of the Novel," Louis

D. Rubin, Jr., described his sense that the most interesting writers (at that hour of the world) were in the process of struggling against a "whole way of using language . . . a whole way of giving order to experience," which had been imposed on the sensibility of the times by the great writers of the immediate past. Rubin went on to predict, "What we are likely to have . . . is a period lasting as long as a full generation or more in which our better writers are more or less engaged, however unintentionally, primarily with learning to see things in their own right again, or at any rate sufficiently in their own right so that what they produce is no longer importantly compromised by the *version of reality* afforded them by their great immediate predecessors" (italics mine).

The startling change in the literary climate that has taken place since that prediction was made, a surprisingly short time ago, strikes me as having occurred in precisely the same way that Louis Rubin described it as likely to happen—except that it has come about with greater swiftness than anyone might have guessed. In the interval, since Susan Sontag, for instance, complained in "Against Interpretation" (1964) that "the sense of what might be done with *form* in fiction" written by Americans is "rudimentary, uninspired, and stagnant," the now-obvious ground swell in American fiction of the last decade has been characterized by incredible transformations of sensibility and language and by a great variety of formal and technical exploration and sophistication. Generalizations about this new fiction are dangerous—it is a process still in motion—but suddenly writers have emerged who face us with compelling new "versions of reality"—more aesthetically advanced though no less stylized than "realism," highly contemporaneous, and written in decidedly idiosyncratic, imaginative, and personal idioms. Fiction, until recently that most *arrière-garde* of contemporary art forms, may suddenly be in the process of catching up with painting, music, and film—may suddenly be in the process of catching up with the age.

The purpose of this book has been to try to find out why this change has taken place and what, in specific terms, has characterized (and is likely to characterize) the transformations of sensibility, language, and formal and technical modes of the present and immediately upcoming periods. The *means* has been to focus on those American writers of the present moment—all either well known or with rising reputations, those who seem to be most involved in effecting significant change, whose artistic innovations, impressive or exotic sensitivities, and/or critical formulations or aesthetic theories seem most compelling, provocative, or influential —and to interview them.

The interview form is characteristic of the age. In its taped form it has technological roots, its expanding popularity a consequence of purely technological breakthroughs of various sorts: miniaturization, videotape, the cassette revolution, and so on. In the immediacy of its appeal to our voracious appetite for personality and glamour, for human contact, for character revelation, for getting-it-from-the-horse's-mouth, it has become a mainstay of *Playboy* and *Rolling Stone*; of Dick Cavett, David Frost, and all the "talk shows"; of *Meet the Press*; of Buckley's *Firing Line*; and, of course, of news journalism generally.

In its temporal (and even spatial) manifestations, the interview form has the fragmentary, simultaneous, discontinuous aspect of television viewing. It allows real time and the time of the medium (reel time) to coincide, a characteristic shared by any number of contemporary fictions and films.

Yet interviews, undoubtedly, have a dubious status as criticism. For one thing, they seem too easy—just a lot of talking written down, or worse—merely gossip. But who could deny the inestimable value of, say, the tapes made of William Faulkner's classes at the University of Virginia (published as *Faulkner in the University*) or of the extremely valuable *Paris Review* interviews? Rigorously intelligent, closely edited interviews, wherein the participants are interested in substantially more than the-writer-as-movie-star-or-pop-astrologer, can prove to be valuable and unique literary artifacts.

While it is a truism that the artist himself, the practitioner, is apt to be a violent or unsystematic critic—and also a propagandist for his own kind of art—the history of criticism reveals again and again the important influence of such violent criticism. Though lacking the judicial impartiality and comprehensive perspective of the pure critic, such commentary, as it approaches criticism, is crucial to the formulation of new principles of understanding. For systematic criticism always lags behind the groundbreaking efforts of live practitioners. Since live practitioners are seldom canonized, academic critics, in dealing particularly with canonized writers, tend to betray a singular obtuseness in the presence of the art of their contemporaries—the contemporary work they approve of (let alone know about) being that which most nearly resembles the work of the past. "Every great and original writer," wrote Wordsworth, "in proportion as he is great or original, must create the taste by which he is to be relished." "If you wanted to know something about an automobile," wrote Pound, "would you go to a man who had made one and driven it, or to a man who had merely heard about it?"

"I began to write fiction," John Hawkes said in an interview in the early sixties, "on the assumption that the true enemies of the novel were plot, character, setting, and theme, and having once abandoned these familiar ways of thinking about fiction, totality of vision or structure was really all that remained. And structure— verbal and psychological coherence—is still my largest concern as a writer." Presumably, in some such fashion, every writer becomes his own aesthetician. He may not be the best authority on his own work—he almost certainly cannot be—but he is still *some sort* of authority if only owing to his inherent position of possessing privileged information. Thus, though an interview may be lacking in systematic rigor or a distanced perspective, it may make up for that lack by supplying indispensable information about just what eclectic concepts, muscular habits, hearsay, or sheer nonsense a writer has chosen to preserve in his life. It may also provide insight into the nature of a particular writer's sensibility—that smoggy

area of aesthetic distinctions least apt to be revealed by traditional
analytical methods.

In addition to its potential for providing such insights; bits of
lore; technical, theoretical, and aesthetic information; and sometimes violent criticism—and, on occasion, especially in these times,
its ability to serve as a bridge between a "difficult" writer and his
potential audience—the interview form may also encompass some
of the pleasures and principles of fiction. Clearly, an interview is,
in one sense, a dialogue that proceeds according to the same
dynamics as any other dialogue: it must (1) express character, or
(2) advance the action. In this context the "action" often has to do
with abstract ideas, let's say, but these are not necessarily lacking
in dramatic ambience, and in the end character and action are, of
course, inseparable. In other words, interesting writers with interesting ideas often turn out to be interesting people—and sometimes
there is not much one can do to prevent it.

Obviously, no book of this kind can hope to be exhaustive, either
in terms of questions asked and answered or in terms of coverage
of all the writers doing significant work who one might wish to
have included. Boiled down, the problem of selection becomes: As
king, how does one choose among a whole harem of Scheher-
azades? Naturally, I felt obliged to select what I saw as a representative grouping. But I still feel inclined to contemplate with
some wistfulness those who might have been included but weren't,
for one reason or another. What about Robert Coover and Thomas
Pynchon, for example? What about J. P. Donleavy, Rudolph
Wurlitzer, Leonard Michaels, Richard Brautigan, William Burroughs, Stanley Elkin, Evan Connell, Jr., Charles Simmons, Ken
Kesey, James Purdy, George Chambers, Bernard Kaplan, W. S.
Merwin, Robert Boles, Raymond Federman, and Steve Katz? What
about Gilbert Sorrentino, LeRoi Jones, Charles Newman, John
Cheever, Harry Crews, Joseph Heller, Clarence Major, George
P. Elliott, Charles Wright, Joy Williams, William Hjorstberg,

Vance Bourjaily, Reynolds Price, Wright Morris, or John Updike (even *if* they had been willing)? All were sacrificed this time around to the exigencies of time, space, and energy—though I wish it had been otherwise.

Although the unifying concerns of the book are expressed in the types of questions asked each writer, I have thought it best to avoid adhering rigidly to a prepared set of questions applied in blanket fashion, intending instead to encourage the interviews to proceed with as much spontaneity as possible. According to the same working principle, though deeply interested in the comprehensive ideological frames of reference of each writer, I have also allowed myself to be interested in what they might choose to avoid articulating or understanding rationally and simply in *them*— in their habits, in their prejudices as well as their intentions, in their feelings about the medium they are working in, in their sense of who has influenced them, in their sense of what is possible.

Still, a number of overriding, if sometimes implicit, central questions do recur in different forms, and these may be worth repeating here to serve as a kind of précis, guidepost, menu, or roadmap: What characterizes the new fiction? What fictional modes seem most played out or moribund? Which seem most compelling as opportunities for continuing imaginative exploration? What are the nature, function, and possibilities of "character" in fiction at the present moment? What influences from other art forms or from electric media seem significant, and how are these expressed? What is and what *should* fiction be *about*? What is fiction good for; that is, what is the purpose of art? What is the relationship between art and reality? Is there a shared reality which it is the writer's business to imitate, to translate, to interpret, or to "create"?

Of course, as one might imagine, the answers elicited proved *not* to be in unanimous concord. How could they be? I leave to the reader the pleasure, or the task, of determining allegiances, drawing parallels, and sifting through certain philosophical morasses. Let me disclaim any interest in attempting to see connections where none exist or in fabricating yet another movement or school. I am interested simply in collating a body of intelligent commentary about the state of current fictional art. My hope is that the work will be contributive both to a better appreciation of the writers themselves and their work and to a better comprehension of the emerging sensibilities, aspirations, and achievements of writers especially responsive, I think, to the vibrations of a culture hardly resembling that of their predecessors.

JDB

Canton, New York
August, 1974

Acknowledgments

I wish to thank the following people for their help with *The New Fiction*: Ted Solotaroff, Jerry Klinkowitz, David Madden, D. Kenneth Baker, and Frank P. Piskor for their encouragement; George McFarland for believing; Janis Glickstein for clerical assistance; and Connie Bellamy and Carol Siyahi for reading and commenting on parts of the manuscript.

My thanks also goes to the editors of the journals in which the following interviews first appeared in whole or in part: John Barth interview, *New American Review*; Joyce Carol Oates interview, *Atlantic Monthly*; William H. Gass interview, *The Falcon*; Ronald Sukenick interview, *Chicago Review*; Tom Wolfe interview, *Touch*; John Hawkes interview, *Novel*; and Jerzy Kosinski and John Gardner interviews, *fiction international*.

Finally, Saint Lawrence University provided a grant and much continuing support which allowed me to complete this work.

The New Fiction

John Barth

INTERVIEWED BY JOE DAVID BELLAMY

In the air-terminal lobby in Williamsport he was already seated, waiting. Standing up, he was taller than I expected, tougher and ruddier, more loose-jointed and lean through the belly. Still, he was unmistakably John Barth—I realized how my expectations had been skewed by black-and-white dust jacket photos. Except for the corduroy and wide tie, he might have been a brigadier general in the RAF or a balding reincarnation of Sam Clemens with that sense of gravity and barely suppressed joviality and reddish-brown flyaway hair. His conversation was brisk, engaging, and pleasantly articulated in a "Piedmont accent," which, like the place of his birth, Cambridge, Maryland, seems almost-but-not-quite Southern.

The occasion for the interview that came about that afternoon, April 1, was Barth's excursion into Pennsylvania for a symposium date at the 1971 meeting of the Northeast Modern Language Association in Philadelphia and a sandwiched-in appearance at Mansfield State College, where he would read from one of his latest works, a novella entitled *Perseid*—part of a group of novellas he was completing using various mythic stories. Published later as *Chimera*, this collection received the 1972 National Book Award

for fiction. (Other works of fiction by John Barth include four
novels—*The Floating Opera, The End of the Road, The Sot-Weed
Factor*, and *Giles Goat-Boy*—and *Lost in the Funhouse: Fiction
for Print, Tape, Live Voice*.)

During the interview, conducted in Mansfield following his
reading, Barth sipped from a glass of Löwenbräu and never appeared to tire. His processes of thought and expression took off
in sustained leaps without the usual gaps, pauses, and short dribbles
that characterize most people's mental activity.

"There is an interesting balance," Barth remarked at one point,
"between theorizing about what you're doing and doing it. As you
compose, particularly if you have a theoretical turn of mind, you're
likely to be interested in working out any theoretical notions that
you might be afflicted with about the medium you're working in.
But you also know . . . that you work to a large degree by hunch
and intuition, and inspiration, as they say. Then, retrospectively,
you may understand a great deal more in the theoretical way about
what it was that you in fact did, than you understood at the time.
When we talk about it, we're talking retrospectively, so I think
sometimes we give the impression that we're all terribly theoretical
when we sit down at the desk, which of course we aren't."

Such qualifications notwithstanding, John Barth is notable,
among other reasons, for the theoretical sophistication of his work.
In meeting him and talking to him, one quickly begins to appreciate why this is so.

JOE DAVID BELLAMY: What sort of general ideas do you have
about the nature of change in contemporary fiction writing at this
point in history?

JOHN BARTH: History is more or less real, and so there are more
or less real reasons why the arts of the twentieth century don't much
resemble those of the nineteenth, the nineteenth the eighteenth,
the eighteenth the seventeenth, and so forth. On the other hand,
having written fiction for a couple of decades, I'm impressed more
all the time by what seems to me the inescapable fact that literature

—because it's made of the common stuff of language—seems more refractory to change in general than the other arts. I think this is true most specifically of prose fiction, probably because of its historical roots in the popular culture. Tchaikovsky would have a great deal of difficulty digging John Cage or any other serious composers since the first World War—much more trouble than Dostoyevsky would have understanding Saul Bellow or even, for that matter, Nabokov. Dostoyevsky would have trouble understanding *Finnegans Wake*, but then we who come after Joyce do, too. Works like *Finnegans Wake* strike some of us as being, after all, the monumental last cry of a certain variety of modernism and not terribly *consequential*, though impressive in themselves.

The permanent changes in fiction from generation to generation more often have been, and are more likely to be, modifications of sensibility and attitude rather than dramatic innovations in form and technique. Especially in the United States novel, in our century, the landmark works, the landmark writers—I use that adjective deliberately because one distinguishes sometimes between what's excellent and what's historically important—the landmark writers more often than not are not formally or technically innovative. Fitzgerald, Hemingway the novelist, Joe Heller, Ralph Ellison, Phil Roth, Saul Bellow, John Updike—however much we may admire them on some sort of grounds, we don't particularly admire them for dramatic innovations in form and technique. I have to add immediately that these are not my *very* favorite writers; and those who are—Borges, Beckett, and Nabokov, among the living grand masters (and writers like Italo Calvino, Robbe-Grillet, John Hawkes, William Gass, Donald Barthelme)—*have* experimented with form and technique and even with the *means* of fiction, working with graphics and tapes and things, echoing a kind of experimentation that has been going on since the beginning of the century and harks back to such works as *Tristram Shandy*.

But even among these, it seems to me, the important difference from their predecessors is more a matter of sensibility and attitude than of means. What the writers that I just mentioned share (except

Robbe-Grillet) is a more or less fantastical, or as Borges would say, "irrealist," view of reality, and this irrealism—not antirealism or unrealism, but irrealism—is all that I would confidently predict is likely to characterize the prose fiction of the 1970s. I welcome this (if it turns out to be, as a matter of fact, true), because unlike those critics who regard realism as what literature has been aiming at all along, I tend to regard it as a kind of aberration in the history of literature.

BELLAMY: What possible directions, then—of a formal or technical nature—do you see contemporary fiction going in?

BARTH: It's going in all directions, including what might appear to be certain retrograde directions. One sees, on the one hand, genuine experiments: concrete fiction, for example—the attempt to devise a narrative equivalent to concrete poetry. I've seen some striking examples of that, and of various kinds of three-dimensional fiction, action fiction, experiments with tapes, graphics, and the like.

On the other hand, just as painting in a certain period of history defines itself against still photography, so it may be that the particular aspects of literature that can't be duplicated in any other medium (especially the cinema), such as its linearity, for example, and its visual verbality, and its translation of all sense stimuli into signs, are precisely the ones that we should pay the most attention to. That is, instead of trying to defeat time, for example, successive time, in narrative, as some writers have attempted in the twentieth century, perhaps we should *accept* the fact that writing and reading are essentially linear activities and devote our attention as writers to those aspects of experience that can best be rendered linearly— with words that go left to right across the page; subjects, verbs, and objects; punctuation!— instead of trying to force the medium into things that are not congenial to it. I say this with all sorts of reservations, because I *am* interested in formal experimentation.

The trick, I guess, in any of the arts at this hour of the world, it to have it both ways. That is, one more or less understands why the history of art, including the art of fiction, has led it through certain kinds of stages and phases to where we are now, and one does ill to deny that history or pretend that it hasn't happened. That's like pretending that the eighteenth century, nineteenth century, and early twentieth century didn't happen.

At the same time, just as one might come to the conclusion that to be linear is not necessarily to be wicked, one may appreciate that because an idea originates in the nineteenth century or eighteenth century it is not necessarily a vicious idea in the twentieth century. And so if I were a composer, for example, I would try to find a way to be absolutely contemporary, insofar as my musical means are concerned—to address myself to the whole history of twentieth-century music, as well as the centuries preceding—and yet write beautiful melodies. (I don't like very much contemporary music as well as I like eighteenth- and nineteenth-century music. I can study it and find it interesting, but it doesn't move me very deeply.) If I were a painter in 1972, I would try to find some way to assimilate all the historical reasons that produce Frank Stella, let's say, and at the same time paint nudes, because one loves nudes.

Now the equivalent of that in fiction would be to find a way to assimilate what's gone before us in the twentieth century—Joyce, Beckett, Borges, and the rest—and yet tell stories, which is an agreeable thing to do. So, if one takes that to be the problem—how to have it both ways—then I think one can see why it is that fiction goes off in our time in some of the directions in which it's going.

BELLAMY: In the mid-sixties Louis D. Rubin wrote an article for the *Kenyon Review* called "The Curious Death of the Novel," in which he talked about the literary climate at that time. He said that the reason the novel was "dead" was that all the great novelists had died, and the critics believed that *those* were "the modern novelists." Since those particular writers had died, the critics thought the novel was dead, too. Rubin ended up saying *he* didn't think the novel was dead at all, of course.

One observation he made about you—you may have read it (this was after *The Sot-Weed Factor*)—was that you had gone back and explored the eighteenth-century novel, taking it as far as it can go.

But then, an implication of his praise was that favorite old saw of American criticism: now we are waiting for the big book [laughter from Barth]. What was the motivation behind *The Sot-Weed Factor*? Do you think *Giles Goat-Boy*, being as it seemed to be yet another new direction for you—a movement toward greater ir-realism—might possibly have been the sort of book Rubin was asking for? And then, how do these books figure generally in the death-of-the-novel controversy?

BARTH: Well, the *Goat-Boy* may or may not be the one Louis Rubin was looking for. It may or may not have been a successor to *The Sot-Weed Factor*. But it is true that one of the things you may be doing as you go through your bibliography, as when you go through your life, is following out certain lines of thought apart from what you're saying overtly.

Thomas Mann remarks that what a writer is writing *about* is seldom the main point; it's what he's doing with his left hand that really matters. *The Sot-Weed Factor* was composed, along with all the other reasons, with certain things in mind about the history of the novel, including the history of my own novels. My first two novels were very short and relatively realistic. By the time I began to compose *The Sot-Weed Factor*—apart from all my other motives and accidental reasons for being interested in that story, like the fact that I grew up near Cook's Point where the real Ebenezer Cook *did* have an estate—I was more acquainted with the history of literature than I'd been when I began to write fiction. And so I set about to untie my hands; I presumptuously felt them tied by the history of the genre and, less presumptuously, by the kinds of things that I myself had been writing before.

One thing I did was move from a merely comic mode to a variety of farce, which frees your hands even more than comedy does. But there was another impulse, which I understood better retrospective-ly—to sort of go to the roots of the novel and see whether I could bring back something new. The eighteenth-century literary conventions were appropriate in part because the eighteenth century and the seventeenth were the centuries when the part of the world that I was writing about became established in European history and imagination. The theme of European innocents coming into America and the theme of the virgin poet—who is not really a poet as long as he is innocent, and who becomes one when he loses his innocence—were congenial.

But the possibility of constructing a fantastically baroque plot appealed to me most: the idea of turning vigorously against the modernist notion that plot is an anachronistic element in contemporary fiction. I've never found that a congenial notion; it seemed to me that there were ways to be quite contemporary and yet go at the art in a fashion that would allow you to tell complicated stories simply for the aesthetic pleasure of complexity, of complication and unravelment, suspense, and the rest. I don't think you could do it with a long face: you would almost have to be parodying the genre in some respect to bring it off. But I don't believe that that is necessarily a sterile or unproductive thing to do. I don't think that it is a particular sign of decadence, especially in the novel, because (as Leslie Fiedler is fond of saying) the novel has always been dying. It was "dying" from the time it was conceived, and it begins in parody. Not just with Fielding, whom I was parodying to some extent—I mean Fielding parodying Richardson—but with Cervantes parodying the chivalric romances. The first novels that we have are already parodies of things in the literary tradition; the mode seems congenial to the genre.

BELLAMY: So you are not pessimistic about the waning of the novel? You wouldn't advise all young writers to go out and become film makers?

BARTH: When I see a young man taking up the practice of fiction as a vocation in this age of the camera, it seems to me that he is doing a very quixotic thing to dedicate his mortal time to that possibly dead art form. But what better adjective! If it is a "quixotic" thing to do, then he's right where the genre begins! So while one writes fiction now in a sort of apocalyptic ambience, it doesn't finally matter at all to the art of literature whether historically this particular little genre fades away. After all, literature got along very well without the novel for most of its history. It comes into existence at a particular time because of particular social and technological conditions; if they no longer obtain and the novel as we know it passes out of literary history there is no great tragedy for anybody. It doesn't mean the end of narrative literature, certainly. It certainly doesn't mean the end of storytelling. The cinema can do some things *like* the novel, but in language, in words, one can do things one can't do in the cinema. And one can do them in ways that have very little to do with the classical novel.

BELLAMY: This begins to sound like a convincing raison d'être for your experiments in *Lost in the Funhouse*. How is it that you turned to *Fiction for Print, Tape, Live Voice* and your continuing preoccupation with myth?

BARTH: It's that aforementioned impulse to investigate the roots that has led some of us in the last few years to explore the possibilities of electronic tapes. That's a way of having it both ways. In some aspects, tapes get us back to the oral tradition out of which literature comes. You have the authorial voice, after all, telling the stories when you work on tape. On the other hand, unlike purely oral literature, a tape has some of the virtues of print: it's interruptable and referable. You can stop a tape, as you can't stop a live storyteller, and you can go back to a particular point—two things that you *can* do on the page that you can't do in the movie theatre, for example, and that you couldn't do with the live oral tradition very easily.

And the same impulse—to find ways to have it both ways—has led some of us too to deal with received stories, particularly the myths. I always felt that it was a bad idea on the face of it, though there are beautiful counter-examples, to write a more or less realistic piece of fiction, one dimension of which keeps pointing to the classical myths—like John Updike's *Centaur*, or Joyce's *Ulysses*, or Malamud's *The Natural*. Much as one may admire those novels in other respects, their authors have hold of the wrong end of the mythopoeic stick. The myths themselves are produced by the collective narrative imagination (or whatever), partly to point down at our daily reality; and so to write about our daily experiences in order to point up to the myths seems to me mythopoeically retrograde. I think it's a more interesting thing to do, if you find yourself preoccupied with mythic archetypes or what have you, to address them directly.

BELLAMY: That's certainly what you seem to be doing in the *Perseid*. How does that work exactly?

BARTH: Well, for example, when I felt at one point in my tape experiments that after all there's something narcissistic about this business of exploiting the authorial voice, my response was to write a story about the myth of Narcissus and Echo, instead of writing a realistic story that echoes narcissism. At the same time, I made the story into a metaphor for the condition of working with tapes.

Echo in the classical myth begins as a girl with a body and her own voice, who can say what she wants to. She's a storyteller, and Zeus hires her to tell stories to his wife, Hera, to distract her with fiction so that he can slip out and make love to other women. Echo does this, and Hera punishes her by taking away her ability to say what she wants to say; she can only repeat the words of others, but she still does it in her own voice, and she still has a body. When she falls in love with Narcissus and her love is not requited, she pines away (we're told in the original myth) until she has no more physical presence at all. She becomes only a voice, her voice, echoing what other people say.

Now in my story, called "Echo," she has passed through one more stage of refinement so that she's lost her individual voice, with its own timbre and inflection, and she has no body anymore. She only repeats what others say, in their own voices—which is what a tape machine does. Echo, at that point, becomes a kind of proto-Ampex. Now the idea was to devise a story about Echo and Narcissus and Tiresias the prophet—who is involved in this myth, too, and who can see backwards and forwards in time—the plot of which would be arranged so that it would be impossible to say, listening to the story on the tape, whether it's Echo telling the story in Tiresias' voice, for example, or in Narcissus' voice, or whether Narcissus is telling the story about Echo, et cetera. Finally, of course, it's the *author's* voice you're hearing, and the author is always all of those things he makes up, so the metaphor becomes rigorously applicable to the conditions of the fiction. Do you understand what I mean?

BELLAMY: Yes. In fact, it strikes me that this is a complex version of the kind of story—and there are a lot of these now by a lot of writers—which tends to start talking about the formal nature of the story and the process of its composition.

BARTH: Exactly. The process is the content, more or less.

BELLAMY: I'm thinking of other examples in *Lost in the Funhouse* which do that in different ways. Do you think there's a basic conflict between that kind of anti-illusionistic writing and the storytelling impulse? That is, when you start talking about the equipment of the story and deliberately break the illusion of the story, do you possibly disrupt the impulse you have toward storytelling and forego those qualities?

BARTH: No, I don't think there's a conflict, only a kind of tension, which can be used. When we talk about it this way it all sounds dreadfully self-conscious, involuted, vertiginous, dull. In the actual execution it doesn't have to be that at all; it can be charming, entertaining; it can even be illusionist. And it's an ancient idea. It's as old as Greek drama, anyhow—to play on the fact that this is a play that you're watching. And Shakespeare does it constantly: "All the world's a stage," et cetera. *The Tempest* is the example *par excellence*—the master of illusion uncloaking his illusions on one level while maintaining them on another.

In other words, the anti-illusionist aspect can be part of the prestidigitation. And that's not decadence or mere gimmickry; it's a way of getting certain kinds of things expressed. Borges makes the remark that those moments in literature when the characters within a work begin to comment on, or be aware of, the fiction that they're in disturb us because such moments remind us of the fiction that *we're* in. A Schopenhauerian idea, which seems to me to be unexceptionable.

The trick, always, is to be at the same time entertaining. I still regard literature as a form of pleasure; and while there are lots of pleasures, including the pleasure of vertigo, I myself like a kind of fiction that, if it's going to be self-conscious, is at least comic about its own self-consciousness. Otherwise, self-consciousness can be a bloody bore. What is more loathsome than the self-loathing of a self one loathes?

BELLAMY: Getting back to the subject of myth, I would be interested in your response to this passage from Robert Scholes' book, *The Fabulators*: "Some influential critics have been ready to proclaim a new age of myth as the most likely literary development of the immediate future. But this, it seems to me, is the least likely of literary developments. [Barth is laughing.] Once so much is known *about* myths and archetypes, they can no longer be used innocently. Even their connection to the unconscious finally becomes attenuated as the mythic materials are used more consciously. All symbols become allegorical to the extent that we understand them. Thus the really perceptive writer is not merely conscious that he is using mythic materials: He is conscious that he is using them consciously. He *knows*, finally, that he is allegorizing. Such a writer, aware of the nature of categories, is not likely to believe that his own mythic lenses really capture the truth. Thus the use of myth will inevitably partake of the comic."

BARTH: That seems to me to be simply the truth.

BELLAMY: Right. Then he goes on and says finally that the modern writer's predicament is that he "knows too much." And this is precisely what keeps his perspective from being seriously mythic.

BARTH: I see his point. I'm not quite sure I agree with it, except as a description of the problem and of the *likely* results. It certainly explains why most of the pieces of literature which resort directly to mythic materials, classical mythic materials, and are at the same time moving and touching and effective for us tend to be comic, or satiric, or parodic literature. This doesn't necessarily mean, however, that they're not passionate or impassioned, in the same way as *Don Quixote*, which begins as a parody of a certain literary genre but soon transcends all that. What Scholes says doesn't rule out the genuinely mythopoeic; it only puts it underground and makes it come in in other places.

Certainly the problem of knowing too much, in the sense in which Scholes speaks of it here, is real. One remembers how writers of the early twentieth century reacted to their awareness of that problem: those writer figures in Thomas Mann, for example, who reach a point where they decide they don't want to understand any more about what they're doing; they turn their back on knowledge in order to keep producing—a kind of counter-Faustian notion. Everybody who writes stories and poems, if he happens to have read a few things as well, confronts this problem: the danger of understanding too much about what he's up to. It's like the problem of being perfectly psychoanalyzed. Many artists resist that kind of understanding of themselves lest it hamper their progress. We know that the things that lead us to get our work done are most imperfectly understood at best, and perhaps had better be left alone lest tinkering with the machinery, or even looking at it too closely, impede its operation.

But it would be foolish to imagine that the collective mythopoeic energy, if one can use that term, is greater or less from one generation, or from one century, to another. I think it simply has to take different forms. And some kinds of writers have it, and others don't, regardless of their other merits and demerits. Henry James is not a very mythopoeic writer. Dickens is a tremendously mythopoeic writer. Of course, when you consciously use an old myth, a received myth, like the myth of Perseus or the myth of Helen, Paris, and Menelaus, then whatever there is of the originally mythopoeic in your own imagination is either going to come in somewhere else in that text—with new characters, or language, or new twists to the old myth—or else will simply flow in to fill in those mythic receptacles which go by the names of Paris, Menelaus, Helen. I believe firmly, in other words, that some of the serious affect that we experience in the face of genuine myth can be experienced in the face of contemporary "comic" fiction using mythic materials.

BELLAMY: Would you say that contemporary writers are ever

able to create their own myths? Or would you say that it's *possible* to create myths?

BARTH: It's a presumptuous thing to aspire to, perhaps—to really make a new myth. And I don't know very much about the scholarly discipline of mythology. But some literary critics and students of myth—Philip Young, for example—will classify, upon occasion, certain works of individual authors, like Irving's *Rip Van Winkle,* as genuine myth. Occasionally it happens! My colleague and friend at Buffalo, Leslie Fiedler, has written a great deal on the subject of the element of the mythopoeic in individual authors, particularly American. I find the things he says on this subject very impressive.

Now a novel like *Giles Goat-Boy,* on the other hand, is not in any sense an attempt to make up a new myth. Not at all, you know. That's a novel that illustrates what Scholes was talking about. When I wrote *The Sot-Weed Factor* I wasn't as aware of certain mythic patterns as I was made aware of them consequently, or subsequently, by the reaction of certain critics and reviewers and students who knew more about comparative mythology than I did. Once one is made aware of the patterns, then the problem is how to be conscious of what one's doing, which can be a fruitful thing, without being in an inhibitory way *self*-conscious about what one's doing—in other words, to avoid being paralyzed by your own knowledge. What I did in the case of the *Goat-Boy* novel was to try to abstract the patterns and then write a novel which would consciously, even self-consciously, follow the patterns, parody the patterns, satirize the patterns, but with good luck transcend the satire a little bit in order to say some of the serious things I had in mind to say. Otherwise it would be a farce, a great trifle—which, of course, some readers found it to be. But the intention was to escalate the farce, to escalate the parody, until the thing took on a genuine dramatic dimension of its own. This may not be making up a new myth, but it's getting to a dimension of response that we can associate with myth, through a comical and farcical mode.

BELLAMY: You said in a previous interview that "there are deep metaphysical reasons why we need more Fielding-like books today with plots where everybody turns out to be related to everybody else...."

BARTH: Did I say that?

BELLAMY: Maybe you were writing *The Sot-Weed Factor* when you said that.

BARTH: Or probably I had just written it and needed to justify it to my own imagination [laughs]. I can't even remember making that comment. . . . But I spoke already of the business of plot as a rather exact equivalent of the element of melody in music. And I like plot in fiction in the same way that I like melodic music. The history of melody—how could you say that?—the Dun and Bradstreet rating of the element of melody in music parallels very carefully the Dun and Bradstreet rating of the element of plot in fiction. Plot goes out of fashion at the same time that melody goes out of fashion. And melody may come back into music by the back door— popular music taken seriously by nonpopular musicians and composers. And story may get back into fiction by that same kind of door. The kids are all turned on by science fiction now, which, whatever else it is, is usually very tight in plot.

BELLAMY: How do you come to terms with the arguments made by Robbe-Grillet and Nathalie Sarraute, and others, that such elements as plot, character, omniscience, and so on, are obsolete notions based on metaphysical assumptions that are no longer applicable?

BARTH: One could say, of course, that the complicated plot in which everything works out and resolves itself in the end belongs historically to centuries where not necessarily the writer but the writer's audience more or less believed in some kind of destiny or fate that saw that things worked out. In other words, periods when one could take a dramatistical view of one's own life—where one's fortunes followed from one's character, and one's relations worked out more or less appropriately, as they should. You could say that the age of the plotted novel belongs to the age when people took that more seriously than they *can* take it in the twentieth century.

Agreeing with all that, I'd still say that if you reject these devices on those grounds, you're operating from an absolutely realist argument. It would be the premises of realism, in other words, that would object to a literary convention for those reasons. Do you follow me? One can think of a lot of twentieth-century French fiction, for example, as being a more subtle kind of realism; instead of being social realism, or psychological realism, the fiction of Robbe-Grillet or Nathalie Sarraute is a kind of epistemological realism. It's the processes of consciousness that are being duplicated, a higher and hi-er fi to the processes of knowing and perception, achieved with more and more sophisticated literary woofers and tweeters.

But another way to address that state of affairs is to regard fiction as artifice in the first place. And if you acknowledge and embrace the artificial aspect of art, which you can't get rid of anyway, then it doesn't necessarily follow, for example, that you have to abandon certain kinds of literary devices simply because they're metaphors for notions that are no longer viable. If you are working in the comic mode, you may be free *ipso facto* to make use of all sorts of conventions because you're parodying them. Your tracks are covered as far as the Robbe-Grillet argument is concerned, and at the same time you can exploit the outmoded conventions for all they're worth to get certain things done that you just can't get done in any other way. . . .

Certainly it's true that a plotted novel is rigorously unrealistic.

BELLAMY: How would that argument go using an example from character as well as plot?

BARTH: One of Robbe-Grillet's points, which I believe he borrows from Roland Barthes, is that the novel of character, such as *Madame Bovary*, for example, or Tolstoy's work, belongs to the *age* of character, to the age of the individual. And in mass society, for example, when individualism as a philosophy is historically discredited, the novel of character is a kind of anachronism. I find that to be a most persuasive argument, but I note to myself that, for example, the simple device of telling a story in the first person obviates almost all those objections.

What I mean is that you and I still imagine ourselves to be

characters, and our lives are influenced by other people around us whom we see as characters and our relations to whom we perceive in a dramatic, in a dramatical, way. As individuals we still live in calendar and clock time; and no matter how that time may be discredited by physicists, it's nevertheless the kind of time we live in during most of our waking experiences. "Microscopes and telescopes," Goethe says simply, "distort the natural focus of our eyes." The metaphysics of cause and effect, for example, may be extremely debatable. But the fact is that we live our lives most of the time with a very simple, crude, and perhaps old-fashioned understanding of cause and effect. We *have* to.

Now, if you write a novel with an "I" narrator, none of these things that Robbe-Grillet objects to as being obsolete or anachronistic can be charged against the *author*, because they only reflect the anachronistic presuppositions of a first-person narrator, who is no more responsible for them than the rest of us are as we go through our lives. So such a simple device as working in the first person, such a simple premise as the comic mode, or the parodic mode, or a fantastical mode, rather than a realistic mode, already, it seems to me, unties you, sets you free from some of these objections—which otherwise are quite compelling.

BELLAMY: What sort of discipline do you set for yourself? Is it regular?

BARTH: Yes, I'm regular. I've not known many prose writers who weren't. It's a tedious vocation, and it takes lots and lots of time. It certainly is a solipsistic and hermit-like thing to do—to close oneself in a room for hours at a stretch, day after day after day, not in human company, listening only to the sound of your own words. Little wonder that one gets interested in stories of people who turn into the sound of their own voices or into their own stories. One of the things that make university teaching valuable to me is that I would simply go buggy if I had nothing else to do but write every day. I think that the absence of other connections with society, with the rest of the world, would be damaging....

BELLAMY: What is your writing schedule like?

BARTH: A prose writer has to have big blocks of time. My wife teaches public school, and she gets up so early to go to work. I usually get up when she does, about 6:00 or 6:30 in the morning, and put an electric percolator full of coffee on in the kitchen just for the excuse of later movement. You know, when you sit for five or six hours your muscles just scream for movement. So I interrupt myself constantly, and I keep the coffee pot plugged in the kitchen when it could just as easily be plugged in the study—so that I can walk back and forth. I drink about six or seven cups between breakfast and lunch, which is really too much caffein. I've tried bouillon, just as something that would be healthier than coffee. But the trouble with that is it's so good you feel as though you're eating lunch, whereas coffee you don't notice. Smoking's probably the answer. I quit that a long time ago. I used to use Dexamyl a lot, and I still do sometimes. You may have found that when you've been working on a long project like a novel—a couple of years, say, and you know early in the game where it's got to go, and it's just a matter of getting there sentence by sentence—I find that I get very drowsy over the manuscript sometimes—very unalert. I don't like that, and I'd either have to quit working earlier than I wanted to— when I got to two hours and I wasn't feeling fresh—or resort to some chemical assistance. My doctor, who is a very leery man, gave me a very mild prescription for Dexamyl, which is a gentle amphetamine plus a kind of tranquilizer. I really am antichemical, and I found that I was so suggestive to these chemicals that I only needed to use half of one a day. He said I could use two or three.

BELLAMY: Did you notice any ill effects at all?

BARTH: Not ill effects. Did you ever use Dexedrine? They all have a similar—speeding—effect. You feel as though you have this endless energy when, in fact, you're just draining your energy. And everything looks interesting to do, and so unless you're very well disciplined—and I think I am—you may end up dissipating this rush of energy in a million other projects besides writing. You may plan four other novels, or find that you really want to change the snow tires on the car. Nothing looks like too much trouble to do.

I went through a period in the late 1950s and early '60s of experimenting with psychic energizers—to keep you working at what you feel is your freshest form for extended periods of time. It scares me now, although I wasn't a very radical experimenter. I came to the conclusion that it's better to be worn out and lose writing days than to keep pushing your sensibility with chemicals that you really don't know very much about. . . .

BELLAMY: One last question. In your essay on Borges, called "The Literature of Exhaustion," you said *The Sot-Weed Factor* and *Giles Goat-Boy* are novels which "imitate the form of the Novel by an author who imitates the role of Author." What did you mean by that?

BARTH: I mean that's strictly correct. One of the interesting things about eighteenth-century fiction, about the early novel, is that the author with a capital *A*, that fellow who intrudes . . .

BELLAMY: Oh, *that* author. You don't mean *you* as an author.

BARTH: Yes, I don't mean that I'm presuming to a medium that I have no business mucking around in [laughter]. Though there are not wanting people who say that that's the case too.

We have such a long history, in the history of fiction, of novels that pretend to be anything but novels. The novel starts that way. *Don Quixote* pretends to be an historical record translated by the Cid Hamete Benengeli, and Richardson's novels pretend to be the letters of Pamela or Clarissa. Fielding's novels pretend to be this, that, or the other thing—anything except that it should be a piece of *fiction*! And in the modern tradition we have novels masking as everything: novels masking as diaries; novels, like that beautiful one of Nabokov's, *Pale Fire*, pretending to be a poem with pedantic footnotes, and so on.

I thought it might be interesting to write a novel which simply imitates the form of the novel, rather than imitating all these other kinds of documents. In other words, it pretends to be a piece of fiction.

Joyce Carol Oates

INTERVIEWED BY JOE DAVID BELLAMY

"I feel a certain impatience with generalizations, especially my own," Joyce Carol Oates wrote in her reply to my preliminary questions, mailed off to her just a few days before, "but I'll try to think out coherent answers to your questions.

"Art is mostly unconscious and instinctive; theories obviously come later in history, in personal history, and are therefore suspicious. Any kind of verbal analysis of any kind of impulsive art is dissatisfying. This isn't a way out of answering difficult questions —though I am always eager to find a way out of questions of any kind—but something I believe in very strongly."

Unlike her previous letter, written out in her careful, elegant hand—in which she gave her consent to this interview by mail—this letter was crowded onto the page, typewritten single-spaced in shotgun style with X-ed-out corrections, almost without margins, as if the pages themselves had seemed scarcely large enough to the writer to contain the potential deluge of language—or so I imagined.

This was not the first time I was to be surprised by the promptness of her replies. I was undecided whether to be gratified by this swiftness or simply flabbergasted. Surely she had more pressing

things to do than to write to me. Surely she *was* attending to those
pressing matters, whatever they were, in addition to writing these
letters. Such productivity struck me as mildly terrifying.

But it was hardly out of character. Winner of the 1970 National
Book Award for fiction, as well as numerous other prizes for her
writing through the years, Joyce Carol Oates has been producing
work (especially fiction, but also poetry, plays, criticism, and reviews) at an astounding rate since the publication of her first
collection of stories, *By the North Gate*, in 1963: six novels—*With
Shuddering Fall, A Garden of Earthly Delights, Expensive People,
Them, Wonderland*, and *Do with Me What You Will*; three more
collections of stories—*Upon the Sweeping Flood, The Wheel of
Love*, and *Marriages and Infidelities*; three books of poetry—*Love
and Its Derangements, Anonymous Sins*, and *Angel Fire*; two plays
produced off-Broadway; a book on tragedy—*The Edge of Impos-
sibility*; and on and on.

The interview-by-mail idea came about at the author's suggestion
after I had written and proposed simply "an interview" to be a part
of this book. I was willing to go about this any way she wanted. As
she remarks at one point in the interview itself, for *her*, at least,
"the whole *social* aspect of [person-to-person] interviewing gets
in the way of ideas."

Certainly Alfred Kazin found her highly elusive and shy on his
February, 1971, visit to Windsor, a central point in his "Oates"
article for *Harper's* (August, 1971), in which their somewhat embarrassing encounter is described by Mr. Kazin as a version of the
I-have-been-in-the-lion's-mouth-and-returned story.

One characteristic of the interchange worth mentioning was the
sense of a deadline to be met, especially since the author and her
husband were preparing to leave for Europe in the fall (note the
"trunks to be packed" reference at the end of the interview)—a
sense that the interview needed to be wrapped up by then. But,
more than that, there was my feeling of being in touch with a
supernormal metabolism, a person used to getting things done very
quickly, a tremendous energy (in spite of her remarks to the con-

trary). There was her emphatic sense of mission, not to mention her kindness and fair-mindedness, a sense of her impatience with any irrelevancy, a sense that in all matters she would feel a keener pressure that *this must be brought to completion.*

The interview which follows is an edited version of the correspondence, including all material that seemed pertinent to a consideration of the writer and her work. Aside from a few minor alterations made for the sake of greater coherence or for the accommodation of the material into an interview format, the questions and answers are reproduced as originally written.

JOE DAVID BELLAMY: What are your writing habits? What times of day do you like to write? How many pages do you average—if there is an average? How do you manage to write so much? Is this simply natural facility, or have you cultivated it in some unusual way?

JOYCE CAROL OATES: I don't have any formal writing habits. Most of the time I do nothing, and the fact of time passing so relentlessly is a source of anguish to me. There are not enough hours in the day. Yet I waste most of my time, in daydreaming, in drawing faces on pieces of paper (I have a compulsion to draw faces; I've drawn several million faces in my life, and I'm doomed to carry this peculiar habit with me to the grave). We live on the Detroit River, and I spend a lot of time looking at the river. Everything is flowing away, flowing by. When I'm with people I often fall into a kind of waking sleep, a day-dreaming about the people, the strangers, who are to be the "characters" in a story or a novel I will be writing. I can't do much about this habit. At times my head seems crowded; there is a kind of pressure inside it, almost a frightening physical sense of confusion, fullness, dizziness. Strange people appear in my thoughts and define themselves slowly to me: first their faces, then their personalities and quirks and personal histories, then their relationships with other people, who very slowly appear, and a kind of "plot" then becomes clear to me as I figure out how all these people came together and what they are doing. I can see them at times very closely, and indeed I "am" them—my personality merges with theirs. At other times I can see them from a distance; the general shape of their lives, which will be transformed into a novel, becomes clear to me; so I try to put this all together, working very slowly, never hurrying the process. I can't hurry it any more than I can prevent it. When the story is more or less coherent and has emerged from the underground, then I can begin to write quite quickly—I must have done forty to fifty pages a day in *Expensive People*, though not every day. Most of the time only fifteen to twenty pages a day. In *Wonderland* [published in October, 1971] I did about the same number of pages on certain days; in fact last summer, working in a kind of trance, elated and exhausted, for many hours at a time. I wasn't creating a story but simply recording it, remembering it. This is true for all of my writing; I have never "made up" a story while sitting at the typewriter.

BELLAMY: What are you working on now?

OATES: This summer [1971] I am putting together a group of short stories called *Marriages and Infidelities*, which includes stories that are reimaginings of famous stories (for instance, "The Dead," "The Lady with the Pet Dog," "The Metamorphosis," "Where I Lived and What I Lived For," "The Turn of the Screw"), and my thoughts are much with this book, when I am able to get them free of *Wonderland*. (If you would like to read "The Dead," retitled by the editors of *McCall's*, it was published in the July [1971] issue of that magazine. "The Turn of the Screw" will be out soon in *Iowa Review* [it appeared in *The Iowa Review*, Vol. 2, No. 2].) These stories are meant to be autonomous stories, yet they are also testaments of my love and extreme devotion to these other writers; I imagine a kind of spiritual "marriage" between myself and them, or let's say our "daimons" in the Yeatsian sense—exactly in the Yeatsian sense, which is so exasperating and irrational!

Now I am in a state of spiritual exhaustion, I think, from the last novel I did, *Wonderland*, a novel about brains—the human brain —which was my most ambitious novel and almost did me in. I had to read a great deal about the human brain, particularly the pathology of the brain; I don't recommend it for anyone. Just going through the galleys brought back to me in a flash all the excitement and dread and exhaustion of those long days last summer when I wrote the novel. I couldn't do it again. It might be my last novel, at least my last large, ambitious novel, where I try to re-create a man's soul, absorb myself into his consciousness, and coexist with him. In my ordinary daily life I am a very conventional person, I think—I hope; but while writing *Wonderland* I found it difficult to keep up the barriers, to keep myself going as Joyce Smith, a professor of English, a wife, a woman, with certain friends, certain duties. It is sometimes such a *duty* to remain sane and accountable. Any study of the human brain leads one again and again to the most despairing, unanswerable questions . . . there is no way out of the physical fact of the brain, no way *out* of this confinement. Yet it can't be measured or adequately explained, at least not the relationship between the brain and the "mind" it somehow generates. It has been months since I've finished *Wonderland*, but I can't seem to get free of it. I keep reliving parts of it, not in the way I still relive *Them* (I was very fond of Jules Wendall, the hero of *Them*) but in another way. It's like a bad dream that never came to a completion. It's the first novel I have written that doesn't end in violence, that doesn't liberate the hero through violence, and therefore there is still a sickish, despairing, confusing atmosphere about it....

BELLAMY: *Wonderland* sounds most intriguing. I was interested in what you said about the ending, how there seems to be a connection between its coming back to haunt you and the fact that it *doesn't* end in violence, doesn't "liberate the hero through violence." Do you have any idea why this is so? Or, for that matter, why violence in general characterizes so much of your work?

Related to this, more specific situations occur to me too—for example, a situation in your work where a man is following a woman or where a woman fears or imagines or even possibly hopes a man is following her (but is at the same time repelled); or a situation where a character might be thinking impulsively of suicide. Why do such situations tend to recur? They are inherently dramatic, obviously. Maybe this is a question you don't care to think about, to become conscious about. I'm asking you to do the critic's job really—or even the psychoanalyst's job—on your own work. That's probably not fair. But I do tend to be curious about it.

OATES: I can't do justice to your question about violence; I can't add much to my fiction on this subject. I don't know. Am I personally haunted by the fear of violence, the need for violence, or do I reflect everyone else's feelings about it? I sense it around me, both the fear and the desire, and perhaps I simply have appropriated it from other people. My own life is quiet, very ordinary and conservative; on a scale of 1 to 10 my own energies (id or otherwise) must be around 2, hovering feebly. I sometimes think of how strange it must be to be a man, burdened with biologically determined energies that no one in his right mind would choose. . . . This is the era of Women's Liberation, but I really must say that I think men have a far more difficult time, simply living, existing, trying to measure up to the absurd standards of "masculinity" in our culture and in nature itself, which is so cruel.

BELLAMY: Coincidentally, I did read your story after "The Dead" in the July *McCall's*. I did catch the Joyce echo, at the end especially, with the snow falling. It is a strong, intriguing, impressive story. (Since Ilena is a writer and so many of the peripheral details of her life seem similar to your own, I did feel somewhat troubled [actually, "embalmed" comes to mind] to learn about her weariness in answering questions about her "writing habits.")

Also, the whole atmosphere of autobiographical confusion—that is, of the mixture of fiction with details that suggested some autobiographical accuracy—was constantly frustrating and amazing and oddly gratifying to my imagination. I suppose it's inevitable that readers develop a sense of curiosity about the personal lives of writers they admire (what else is biography for?). (The question I want to ask here is not, I think, ultimately embarrassing.) Some writers, once they become famous enough (Norman Mailer comes to mind), learn to make good dramatic use of characters similar to or possibly identical to, or even quite different from (but apparently similar to—the reader never knows), themselves. Do you think you were doing something of that sort in this story? (I hope that's a fair question.)

OATES: Some of the details in the story are authentic, some slightly invented, but the general tone of busyness is real enough; except I haven't the aloneness of the character in the story, her freedom to simply be alone once in a while, even if only to think dark thoughts and recall with amazement simpler times.

My use of myself in stories—well, it has always been there, the use of emotions I've felt. I should be a rational, contained person, I guess, but really I am very emotional—I believe that the storm of emotion constitutes our human tragedy, if anything does. It's our constant battle with nature (Nature), trying to subdue chaos outside and inside ourselves, occasionally winning small victories, then being swept along by some cataclysmic event of our own making. I feel an enormous sympathy with people who've gone under, who haven't won even the small victories. . . .

BELLAMY: Questions about writing habits *are* probably futile. The implication of the questions is usually: "Tell me your secret. If I know how to do it, maybe I will be able to do it." All of this preliminary is unnecessary. I want to ask you a few more simple-minded, possibly boring questions about your writing habits, and then I won't bring up the subject again. (a) Do you drink coffee before or while working? If so, how much? (b) Do you sleep well? How many hours a night on the average? Do you remember your dreams well—your nighttime dreams, I mean? (c) Have you ever tried amphetamines or other sorts of stimulants to help you work better? (I'm thinking of Ilena in the *McCall's* story and also John Barth, who said he sometimes uses a very mild form of speed to help him work better.)

OATES: [This is] a very normal question, which you needn't apologize for, [about] the use of drinks, drugs, coffee, and so on. I don't take drugs of any kind, or even drink, or smoke (I'm so dull—see Alfred Kazin's essay on me in the August *Harper's*), or even drink coffee; it's just the way I happened to grow up, nothing essentially puritanical and certainly not moral about it. But I have the idea that I could very easily become addicted to nearly anything —drugs, for instance—because they are a way of taming the emotions, of calming things down, of controlling—at least temporarily —the uncontrollable. I understand absolutely why there are so many people addicted to drugs or alcohol—it would be a surprise if there weren't so many people like this. I am addicted to work, which is to say the expulsion of built-up ideas and formless forms, the need to get rid of little stories that crowd my head. Alfred Kazin was quite right in saying that I sometimes write as if to relieve my mind of things that haunt it, not to create literature that will live. (But I don't think many writers really work consciously to create literature that will "live"—that will be monumental, like *Ulysses*. I think most writers write out of an interior compulsion, hoping that it will add up to an artistic statement of some worth.)

About my dreams: I seem to be always dreaming, awake or asleep, though when I'm awake I *know* I'm awake. I wonder if this is normal . . . ? My husband evidently doesn't experience this. Asleep, I dream about anything, just like anyone else; but I have terrible nights of insomnia, when my mind is galloping along and I feel a strange eerie nervousness, absolutely inexplicable. What a nuisance! Or, maybe it isn't a nuisance? An ideal insomnia allows for a lot of reading. When the house is dark and quiet and the entire world turned off for the night, it's a marvelous feeling to be there, alone, with a book, or a blank piece of paper, even a blank mind, just sitting there alone. Such moments of solitude redeem all the rushing hours, the daylight confusion of people and duties. I like to write, but I really love to read: that must be the greatest pleasure of civilization.

BELLAMY: What *do* you read?

OATES: I read constantly, in three areas—the re-reading of old works (I'm now going through *Ulysses* again); the reading of an avalanche of literary quarterlies, magazines, reviews, and so on, that come into our home steadily (some magazines are not read

but devoured: *New American Review, TriQuarterly*, for instance
—incredibly good magazines); and new novels. There is a vigor
and an excitement in contemporary writing that I think is remarkable. I have only to reach out for any current magazine—let's say
New American Review, which is handy, issue number 10—to discover at least one story that is striking, maybe even a masterpiece.
In this issue of *NAR* it is Philip Roth's "On the Air"—Kafka and
Lenny Bruce and pure Rothian genius, very hard, bitter, terrifying
stuff.

BELLAMY: What about the future of fiction in general? Do you
think the novel may be dead or dying?

OATES: The novel can't be dead or even close to dying if an
American publisher can bring out one good novel a year, just
one—let's say Bellow's *Mr. Sammler's Planet* last year and Doc-
torow's *The Book of Daniel* this year. We would hope for more,
and we usually do get more.

BELLAMY: What sort of possibilities do you see for those fiction
writers who are trying to break out of the conventions of the so-
called realistic tradition? Are you one of these writers?

OATES: Fiction writers have broken out of the "conventions of
the so-called realistic tradition" years ago, decades ago; it's a com-
monplace of critical thought to point all the way back to *Tristram
Shandy* as a convention-breaking work, but even (even!) *Tom
Jones* is rather iconoclastic. There has never been a novel so fantastic
as *Remembrance of Things Past*. It is all things, a complete life, an
extended thought, an arrangement and rearrangement of reality
that is much more believable than the reality of most lives lived
daily, at least in my part of the world. July 10, 1971, was Proust's
one-hundredth birthday, and he is very much alive. Another iconoclastic novel is *Dr. Faustus*. What an accomplishment! I am always rereading Mann in utter admiration, in love. Ah, to be able
to write like Thomas Mann . . . or even to write a novel that Mann
might approve of, even mildly. . . . When I write a story or a novel
I don't feel that I am any particular person, with a particular ego.
I seem to share, however vaguely, in the "tradition"—the tradition

of literature, of all that has been done that I know about and love. Each story has a form and a style that is best suited for it, and all I do is wait around until these things come together—the people in my imagination who are to be the "characters" in the formal work, the form, the style, the language, the setting (which is another character), the mood, the year. So I don't think of myself as "one of those writers who is trying to break free of conventions." There aren't any conventions really. And if *Middlemarch* is a conventional novel, how wonderful it would be if contemporary novelists could write anything comparable! There are no conventions or traditions, only personalities.

BELLAMY: Your statement "There are no conventions or traditions, only personalities" I find very liberating and helpful. But I still worry about that question. Of course, fiction writers broke away from the conventions of the so-called realistic tradition years ago; and, of course, the history of the novel can be seen as a series of rebellions against previously "established" forms—all the way back to the very beginning. But aren't those rebellions still going on? And if it isn't one writer rebelling against a "tradition," maybe it's a personality rebelling against another personality, or simply any writer working to find something new to keep from boring herself or himself to death.

Maybe what I should have asked was: What sort of presently occurring formal innovations interest you the most? Or—Wouldn't you agree that the electric media, for example, have had various sorts of unprecedented influences on contemporary writing? I mean something beyond bothersome prophesies of its demise—formal influences, time-and-space influences? And haven't these affected you? In your own work there seems to be a greater interest in formal experimentation. "The Turn of the Screw" might be one example. In *The Wheel of Love*, stories such as "How I Contemplated the World" and "Matter and Energy," or even "The Wheel of Love" or "Unmailed, Unwritten Letters" (which is much more than a simple epistolary story), seem more formally innovative to me than any of the earlier stories, say, in *By the North Gate*. Why is this?

OATES: I am interested in formal experimentation, yes, but generally this grows out of a certain plot. The form and the style seem naturally suited to the story that has to be told; as in "Matter and Energy" (a story I feel very close to), where the young girl's present life is entirely conditioned by what happened in the past and her love for a man entirely conditioned—ruined—by her love for her mother, a rotten, hopeless love. Think of the horror of existing always with the memory of such a mother—committed to an insane asylum—while "you" are free, evidently, to walk around and to act normal, to try to love, to act out a certain role. One always thinks of a few other people, day after day; there's no escape. A father, a mother, a few beloved people—that is the extent of the universe, emotionally. And if something has gone wrong inside this small universe, then nothing can ever be made right. (This story is based on the anguished recollections of a student of mine whose mother is in an asylum and who tried to kill him, many years ago. He is now an adult, an earnest and intelligent young man, but at the same time he is still that child; he is *still* coming home to that mother, to that event.) So the form of that story grew naturally out of its subject matter.

In "The Turn of the Screw," the use of journals is a kind of Victorian cliché; among other things I wanted to suggest how interior lives touch upon one another in odd, jagged, oblique ways without communicating any essential truth, in fact without communicating truth. In "Unmailed, Unwritten Letters" (which is perhaps my favorite story, at least emotionally) the epistolary form is a way the heroine has of sending out cries for help—not meant to be heard, simply a way of articulating private bewilderment. Not that I want to dwell upon this story, but it seems to have touched some common chord in people—I've received a number of letters from other writers/critics/men of letters of a type who seem to like it. What does this mean about our American marriages . . . ?

BELLAMY: What is your concept of characterization? Or what are your ideas about characterization? This is overly general perhaps. How about this: Do you think "hardened" character such as the kind in Victorian novels is real or valid?

OATES: Your questions about characterization are quite coherent questions, yet I can't answer them because—as you might gather from what I have already said—I don't write the way other people evidently write, or at least I can't make sense of what they say about their writing. My "characters" really dictate themselves to me. I am not free of them, really, and I can't force them into situations they haven't themselves willed. They have the autonomy of characters in a dream. In fact, when I glance through what I have tried to say to you, it occurs to me that I am really transcribing dreams, giving them a certain civilized, extended shape, clearing a few things up, adding daytime details, subtracting fantastic details, and so on, in order to make the story or the novel a work of art. Private dreams have no interest for other people; the dream must be made public, by using one's wit.

People say that I write a great deal, and they are usually curious about when I "find time." But the odd thing is that I waste most of my time. I don't think I am especially productive, but perhaps other writers are less productive. In the past, however, writers like Henry James, Edith Wharton, Dickens (of course), and so on and so forth, wrote a great deal, wrote innumerable volumes, because they were professional writers and writers write. Today, it seems something of an oddity that a writer actually writes, and some writers or critics who don't spend much time writing seem to resent more productive writers. Someone said that John Updike publishes books as often as John O'Hara did, but thankfully his books weren't quite as long as O'Hara's. . . . This is an attitude I can't understand. Any book by Updike is a happy event. The more, the better. If any critic imagines that he is tired of Updike, then he should not read the next Updike novel and he certainly should not review it.

I don't know that the above will strike you as good enough,

or that I have answered your questions. I know one thing, though: I would never have thought of some of these things in a person-to-person interview. The whole *social* aspect of such interviewing gets in the way of ideas.

You are kind in the many things you say about my writing and about me (you probably do know me quite well, because I've told you things that acquaintances and social friends of mine would never be told, not in dozens of years). It may be that I am mysterious, in a way; certainly there are things about myself that don't make sense to me and are therefore mysterious, to me, but the main thing about me is that I am enormously interested in other people, other lives, and that with the least provocation (a few hints of your personal life, let's say—your appearance, your house and setting) I could "go into" your personality and try to imagine it, try to find a way of dramatizing it. I am fascinated by people I meet, or don't meet, people I only correspond with, or read about; and I hope my interest in them isn't vampiristic, because I don't want to take life from them but only to honor the life in them, to give some permanent form to their personalities. It seems to me that there are so many people who are inarticulate but who suffer and doubt and love, nobly, who need to be immortalized or at least explained.

Here in Windsor, life is filling up with people: parents coming to visit, trunks to be packed, last-minute arrangements to be made, a dozen, a hundred chores, such as what to serve for dinner tonight. But thank God for trivial events! They keep us from spinning completely off into the dark, into the abstract universe.

I hope these answers make some kind of sense to you. Much of this I haven't thought out, until now; it sounds bizarre but is very honest.

William H. Gass

INTERVIEWED BY CAROLE SPEARIN MC CAULEY

Most philosophers don't write fiction. Or (if you're a cynic), fictions are all they write.

William Gass is both a philosopher who writes fiction and a writer whose aims and work have been deeply influenced by his philosophical training. His imaginative and experimental use of language and narrative technique in a variety of books has earned him both acclaim and dismissal during the years since parts of his first novel, *Omensetter's Luck*, appeared in *Accent Magazine*. About that book Susan Sontag wrote: "William Gass has written an extraordinary, stunning, beautiful book. I admire him and it very much." Richard Gilman remarked: "William Gass is not a comfortable writer. He's not immediately available. His work yields up new truths of our experience instead of repeating words of the past."

Born in North Dakota in 1924, Gass was educated at Kenyon College and Cornell University (Ph.D.) He is currently professor of philosophy at Washington University, St. Louis. His published works are *Omensetter's Luck* (New American Library, 1966), *In the Heart of the Heart of the Country* (story collection, Harper & Row, 1968), *Fiction and the Figures of Life* (critical essays,

Knopf, 1970), and *Willie Masters' Lonesome Wife* (*TriQuarterly*, 1968, and Knopf, 1971). His literary criticism appears frequently in *New American Review* and *New York Review of Books*. A long excerpt from *The Tunnel*, his work in progress, appeared in *TriQuarterly* No. 20 (Winter, 1971).

I began the following interview in late November, 1971, at the Poetry Center, YMHA, New York City, where Gass was reading. We completed it by mail over the next several weeks and months.

The following quotations are from *Fiction and the Figures of Life*:

". . . [H]ow absurd these views are which think of fiction as a mirror or a window onto life—as actually creative of living creatures...."

". . . [T]here are no events but words in fiction."

"The advantage the creator of fiction has over the moral philosopher is that the writer is concerned with the exhibition of objects, thoughts, feelings, and actions where they are free from the puzzling disorders of the real and the need to come to conclusions about them."

CAROLE SPEARIN MCCAULEY: From your literary criticism (including the above) it seems the philosopher side of you mistrusts the fiction-writing side because the fiction process involves the deliberate telling of lies, the setting forth of actions and people that never happened. How do you reckon with this dilemma?

WILLIAM GASS: I don't distrust the artist as artist at all. I distrust people, including artists, who make pretentious claims for literature as a source of knowledge.

This was the half of Plato's complaint against the poets which I accept. I see no reason to regard literature as a superior source of truth, or even as a reliable source of truth at all. Going to it is dangerous precisely because it provides a sense of verification (a feeling) without the fact of verification (the validating process). Plato was simply too exclusive about his values. He took knowledge to be the supreme good. Consequently he had to banish the poets (for the most part). The appeal to literature as a source of truth is pernicious. Truth suffers, but more than that, literature suffers. It is taken to be an undisciplined and sophistic sociology, psychology, metaphysics, ethics, etc., etc.

When I speak of telling lies, I speak ironically.

McCAULEY: It seems as if you desire your fictional characters to exist as pure essences, as ideas that the reader can apply to his own life, provided he doesn't assume they really exist beyond the page. For example, in *Fiction and the Figures of Life* (page 37) you say, "Though the handbooks try to tell us how to create characters, they carefully never tell us we are making images, illusions, imitations. Gatsby is not an imitation, for there is nothing he imitates." How did you arrive at this position, which puts you squarely against what most writers desire—and against all the advice to young writers to create "real characters in real situations"?

GASS: Most writers? Most writers of what sort? There is some truth to this, but it is also partly a myth about writers spread by critics and other advertisers who know nothing about the art of writing. "The only reality is the translation of one's ideas into rhythm and beautiful movements." Colette is a writer many would expect to be on an opposite side, but she isn't at all, and this is really true for most serious artists.

That advice to young writers—who is giving it? Teachers in writing workshops, journalists, editors, hacks. As a student of philosophy I've put in a great deal of time on the nature of language and belong, rather vaguely, to a school of linguistic philosophy which is extremely skeptical about the nature of language itself.

McCAULEY: In *Fiction and the Figures of Life* you find a "fear of feeling" in the work of some writers in our current literary pantheon such as Hawkes, Barthelme, Coover, Barth, Nabokov, Borges—that they "neglect the full responsive reach of their readers." So if you don't want the reader to "care" in the old sense of where-Hamlet-is-when-he's-not-onpage-or-onstage, then what is it exactly you want the reader to feel?

GASS: I want him to feel the way he feels when he listens to music—when he listens properly, that is. My complaint about Barth, Borges, and Beckett is simply that occasionally their fictions, conceived as establishing a metaphorical relationship between the reader and the world they are creating, leave the reader too passive. But such words are misleading. I have little patience with the "creative reader."

I mean this: some metaphors work in one direction—the predicate upon the subject. When I say that her skin was like silk, I am using the concept silk to interpenetrate and organize the idea of skin. Some metaphors, however, interact—both terms are resonant. If Hardy writes, "She tamed the wildest flowers," then not only has "she" become an animal trainer, the flowers have become animals. Nor has "taming" been left untouched, for such taming is now seen in terms of gardening. Now if fictions are metaphors or models, then perhaps they should occasionally "fictionalize" the reader.

McCAULEY: In the words of Kohler, *The Tunnel's* narrator: "My subject's far too serious for scholarship, for history, and I must find another form before I let what's captive in me out. Imagine: history not serious enough, causality too comical, chronology insufficiently precise." Does fiction writing interest you as the alternative? Like philosophy and Aristotle's "poetry," it can strive after the universal rather than the particular.

GASS: This is Kohler's problem, not mine. History, as I see it, can strive for the universal. My objection to it is simply that it rarely, reasonably, does. Many of my attitudes toward history are expressed by Levi-Strauss. For me fiction isn't an alternative to anything, however, and it doesn't strive for universals. It merely makes particular things out of universals.

History, philosophy, fiction, like mathematics or physics, are for me all equally important, all difficult to do, rarely well done, each requiring its own disciplines, techniques, skills, and very different in aim. When Kohler says his subject is too serious for scholarship, etc., he means it is too personal, that the modes he mentions won't satisfy him. It reflects *his* mood.

McCAULEY: Wittgenstein defines philosophy as "a battle against the bewitchment of our intelligence by means of language." Does this relate to your concerns in fiction or philosophy?

GASS: I think philosophy is more than this, but it certainly should be this. It has often been busy bewitching. Philosophy ought to spend more time than it has showing how little we need it—it and other foolish sets of opinions. I believe much of what has passed for philosophy, theology, etc., in the past is nonsense. Sometimes beautiful nonsense, if you enjoy myths of the mind as I enjoy them. Beliefs are a luxury, and most of them are wicked gibberish.

Philosophical ideas can, however, provide the writer with complex centers of meaning, rich bases to work from. But you must *play* with them primarily because of the danger that what you're saying might be so. Constructing fictions as if the philosophy they're based on *were* so usually leads to falseness.

McCAULEY: How or where did you get the material for the characters and Ohio setting of *Omensetter's Luck*? For example, was Omensetter or Jethro Furber or the father in "The Pedersen Kid" modeled on someone you knew (who actually existed)?

GASS: I made it up. I know nothing whatever of Ohio river towns and care less. The only time I ever used a "model" in writing was when, as a formal device, and to amuse myself, I chose to get the facts about "B" in "In the Heart of the Heart of the Country" exactly right. Models interfere with the imagination. Which is better—to play train with a square wooden block, or a scale model? If you have a model, whether a person or a scene, even an idea, you tend to find yourself bent by that model when the work you are doing at any time should be obedient only to itself. Of course writers get ideas from models all the time and, occasionally, so do I, but they have to be able to leave the given behind. I generally take no chances and work "in the dark"—modelless.

Omensetter isn't really set in Ohio; that is the point.

McCAULEY: In your essay in *Afterwords: Novelists on Their Novels* you wrote, ". . . the illusion might wrap itself like a sheet around its occupant, so that Omensetter might become a ghost even to himself." Did you intend Omensetter to remain the mystery that many people find him—because we never got inside him directly?

Despite Omensetter's "luck," does his baby die?

GASS: Omensetter is a reflector. People use him the way they use their gods or other public figures—like ink blots—and upon them they project their hopes and fears. Who cared to know Omensetter? And when their hopes were dashed, they blamed the image in the mirror. So of course Omensetter is a mystery and he had to be left, in a sense, blank. Readers are now doing to him exactly what the characters in the book did.

No. His baby doesn't die. Omensetter is a lucky man.

McCAULEY: I notice a total difference in tone from something like passionate optimism (people's lives and deaths matter, America matters) in *Omensetter's Luck*, compared to the narrator's disenchantment in *The Tunnel*. How do you explain this?

GASS: The tonal difference is due to the differences in the books. The narrator in *The Tunnel* is disenchanted, but, again, that's his problem. I have always been disenchanted, although I am probably less bitter about things now than I was when I wrote *Omensetter's Luck*. I'm personally happier. But *The Tunnel* will be a very bitter book. I thought *Omensetter's Luck* pretty bitter, too. Also, you've only seen fragments from *The Tunnel*. If you saw more of it, your feeling about the tone might change.

McCAULEY: Do you feel America has lost its Omensetters, the people who know how to live naturally, unintellectually? Why or why not?

GASS: America never had its Omensetters. There aren't any such human felines. Such creatures are a part of the American myth. What we are losing is our belief in such things. Beliefs lost are minds cleaned. I applaud the development.

McCAULEY: You seem to have the kind of mind that brews fiction from massive amounts of stream of consciousness (Jethro Furber, Israbetis Tott). Do you have a method for keeping up the white heat, the Molly Bloom effect?

GASS: No method for "white heat." Whenever I find myself

working at white heat, I stop until I cool off. I write very slowly, laboriously, without exhilaration, without pleasure, though with a great deal of tension and exasperation. I fuss over little bits, scarcely ever see beyond my nose, and consequently bump it constantly.

McCAULEY: Do you do much "research" to complete your fiction, make it real by revisiting "the scene of the crime," hunting out people who resemble your characters, etc?

GASS: No research. I collect words. Twelve different names for *whore* among the Romans. Thirty-five names for cloths and silk stuffs. Etc. Sometimes I even use what I've collected. Or an old book will suggest something. But there are no "scenes" to revisit, except for "B," and I wouldn't think of doing that while writing, because, as I said, my choice of factuality in that case was purely formal. I collected real names of clubs, for example, and amused myself by arranging them. Part of the game was not to invent any. It would have been like cheating at solitaire.

McCAULEY: Do you intend, as part of the fun, that the "Masters" in *Willie Masters' Lonesome Wife* could refer to William Masters of the St. Louis sex research? Or that "Kohler" in *The Tunnel* means "miner" in German?

GASS: I began *Willie* and wrote most of it in 1966, before I'd ever heard of Masters and Johnson. Scarcely before I'd ever heard of St. Louis. The jokes are there—in Goethe, in Shakespeare, etc.

The choice of "Kohler," however, was deliberate. Miner in the tunnel . . . yes.

McCAULEY: Do you have a writing schedule? Are you able to write every day? Do you do any sort of warmup exercises? What do you do if you get blocked?

GASS: I have a schedule for writing whenever I have enough free time that having such a schedule seems realistic—when I'm off because of a grant or during the summer. I used to be able to write nearly every day, but that has become impossible. I don't do warmup exercises, but I do try to stop work only when I've left some fingers pointing to the future—some lines I can begin my next day's work by starting with. If I have to start cold, with entirely new material (new sentences, I mean), then I have trouble.

I don't really get blocked; that is, I don't find that I sit and stare at the page and nothing comes. Not for long. But I have blocks in the sense that I allow things to distract me so that for a long time I won't work. It is the same as a block, though perhaps not so immediately distressing.

McCAULEY: Did you have to write for many years before you succeeded in being published?

GASS: I began writing seriously (I always wanted to write, planned on it, etc.) in 1951. I wrote "The Pedersen Kid" and the opening parts of *Omensetter* in '51–'52. I didn't get published until *Accent* devoted an issue to my work in 1958. *Omensetter* didn't get written for a long time, but it wasn't published until 1966. "The Pedersen Kid" (finished in '51) had to wait until 1961. Even *Willie* waited from 1966 to '68. "In the Heart" waited. They all wait. So that it is generally true that most of my stuff is old when it appears—old to me, that is.

McCAULEY: What do you like to read? Are there any authors you've learned something from?

GASS: I am an omnivorous reader. My library is that of a dedicated dilettante. I might, on any given day, be reading a book about bees, or about epistemology, or about the brain, or about the theory of signs, or about odd native tribes, or odd psychological states, or sexual positions, or who knows—travel, geography, biography. . . . I like letters, diaries, journals, gossip, and therefore history. I read less and less poetry, though I get to Rilke almost every day. I rarely read fiction and generally don't enjoy it. I usually read it because I have to. Lately, most of my reading has been of that sort. I read X because I have to shoot off my mouth about it—teaching, reviewing—and I'm sick of it.

I've learned from so many I couldn't even begin to list the essential. As far as my own writing goes, from poets mostly, from philosophers, of course, because they supply me with material, and from stylists in general, whether Sir Thomas Browne, Hobbes, Stein, Joyce, James, Ford, or Colette.

McCauley: Do you enjoy any of the other arts?

Gass: I enjoy all of them, especially perhaps ballet (when pure and not mucked up) and architecture. I was an opera nut when young. That's tailed off. I haunt museums when I can. In one sense, painting has influenced my theory of art more than almost anything, music my practice of it.

McCauley: Do you write poetry or plays?

Gass: I wrote terrible poetry in my youth. I write doggerel now. I am a rotten poet and have absolutely no talent for it.

I haven't the dramatic imagination at all. Even my characters tend to turn away from one another and talk to the void. This, along with my inability to narrate, is my most serious defect (I think) as a writer and incidentally as a person. I am (though I wasn't especially raised as one) a Protestant, wholly inner-directed, and concerned only too exclusively with *my* salvation, *my* relation to the beautiful, *my* state of mind, body, soul. . . . The interactions which interest me tend to be interactions between parts of my own being. One could, I suppose, try to get a little drama out of that. Besides, the drama is a mug's game. Actors are enemies. The theater is cheap, divided in its source of control. It would drive me crazy.

McCauley: Do political issues on campus or among students interest you for their fictional possibilities? That is, there's terrible pressure on fiction to "be relevant" today, to deal with "today's real issues" instead of rural people or private consciousness. So we have Norman Mailer making his career as a sort of hippy-fascist weathercock telling us how tomorrow's winds will blow in America. How do you deal with this pressure to "be relevant"?

Gass: Art is never concerned with such things. Relevance is meaningless to it. A work of art is made to last as a valuable being in the world. As such it may develop, over time, useful relations to the world; but just as human beings ultimately must find their values in themselves, so works of art must *be relevant by being.* There have always been Mailers because culture requires its human talismans. These procedures and activities are as different from art as weeds from differential equations. I feel no pressure to be relevant.

I am, of course, as a person, interested in these public matters, and I am frequently taken from my work to engage in them. They are, indeed, often far more important than myself and my private playthings. Dante was "relevant," but fortunately he triumphed over it.

McCAULEY: Is teaching a stimulus to your writing, or something that just takes time from it? I know that you received the Hovde Prize for excellence in teaching in 1967.

GASS: It used to be. I think I fed on the students. They have been an enormous help to me in every way, but my interest in teaching grows less—I think mainly because my toleration of the monkey business which attends it grows less. Now I often feel that it just takes time. But I really enjoy lecturing (not teaching); I never really enjoyed teaching. I enjoy talking to the material. And if I'm not doing that aloud, I'm doing it silently. It's nice to get paid for it.

McCAULEY: Someone from the Midwest (even New Jersey!) can feel discriminated against by the New York literary establishment, perhaps criticized for being provincial, unsophisticated, whatever. Has this kind of treatment ever afflicted you?

GASS: When I go to New York City, I feel I'm going to the provinces. What is sophisticated about literary New York? How much of importance goes on there? It is filled with commercial hacks and their pimps. There are, of course, many cultivated people —people who have their values straight, who know even more about Valéry or Péguy, say, than about Mailer or Updike—but most of them mistake the literary froth for the body of the beer.

Literature doesn't take place in New York. It takes place in writers' heads and on their pages all over the world. From the literary point of view New Yorkers live in the servants' quarters. No, I haven't been afflicted. Literature is where the Faulkners are. No Faulkner is in New York, and if he were, he wouldn't be known. I snub them.

McCAULEY: Did you have to submit *Omensetter's Luck* to many publishers before it was noticed by New American Library and other people in New York?

GASS: I think *Omensetter's Luck* went to twelve publishers (so much for New York sophistication). New American Library didn't notice it. It takes no notice of books. David Segal saw the book early on—tried to get it published at McGraw-Hill, finally succeeded at NAL. If it hadn't been for my agent, Lynn Nesbit, and for David, it probably would still be unpublished, and so would all the rest of my stuff.

McCAULEY: Did they suggest or require many revisions?

GASS: David suggested a few revisions—nothing major—most wise suggestions from him. I do my own work and do not permit other people to interfere with it. Editors occasionally ask for cuts, and sometimes I submit to them (for magazine publication). Anyone who requires revisions has simply rejected the manuscript as far as I'm concerned. Some (a few) wanted to do that with *Omensetter's Luck*.

McCAULEY: How do you generally revise your work? Just two drafts or many more?

GASS: I work not by writing but by rewriting. Each sentence has many drafts. Eventually there is a paragraph. This gets many drafts. Eventually there is a page. This gets many drafts. And so on. I have about three hundred pages of *The Tunnel*. But in a few days I start over redrafting them—from the beginning.

Writing isn't easy for me. That's why I have to answer your questions in pidgin, for if I began to worry about what I was saying and the way I was saying it—well, I'd never answer your questions. I would never emerge from number one. So I'm a poor correspondent. I deliberately butcher matters. Write wretchedly. Turn no phrases. Speak telegraphese.

McCAULEY: How do you feel about *The Tunnel* compared with *Omensetter's Luck*? Progression or enlargement?

GASS: *The Tunnel* is a crucial work for me. All my work up to it I have privately thought of as exercises and preparations. This was a dodge, of course, but it did work. How can you fail when you are simply practicing, learning, experimenting? I can't hide behind that dodge any more. Further, in this business it is no honor to finish second. Now I shall find out whether I am any good.

Certainly I hope that *The Tunnel* will be better than *OL*. *OL* made compromises. I trust that *The Tunnel* will not. I hope that it will be really original in form and in effect, although mere originality is not what I'm after.

OL made compromises because it still sometimes treated fiction as if it were an imitation of some factual form. *OL* made only sporadic steps at establishing its own form.

Fiction has traditionally and characteristically borrowed its forms from letters, journals, diaries, autobiographies, histories, travelogues, news stories, backyard gossip, etc. It has simply *pretended* to be one or other of them. The history of fiction is in part a record of the efforts of its authors to create for fiction its own forms. Poetry has its own. It didn't borrow the ode from somebody. Now the novel is imagined news, imagined psychological or sociological case studies, imagined history . . . feigned, I should say, not imagined. As Rilke shattered the journal form with *Malte*, and Joyce created his own for *Ulysses* and *Finnegan*, I should like to create mine.

McCauley: Do you have any advice for beginning writers? Do you recommend fiction writing classes? Would you ever teach creative writing? If so, what would be your approach?

Gass: My advice for beginning writers is first to recognize that writers differ a great deal in their own natures and in the nature of their talent, and that little advice which is general can be of much value. Learn not to take advice. Look to yourself. Make yourself worthy of trust.

No art can be taught, though some techniques sometimes can. Writing classes help some, don't others. It depends again on the kind of person you are. Do whatever works. It wouldn't have worked for me, and I am personally suspicious of them. I've taught creative writing (a little), but I would never make a habit of it. All that attention wasted on poor work? Better to speak of the good things and learn from that. So my approach would be flight.

McCAULEY: Can you estimate when your book *The Tunnel* will be finished or published?

GASS: I began *The Tunnel* in 1966. I imagine it is several years away yet. Who knows, perhaps it will be such a good book no one will want to publish it. I live on that hope.

Donald Barthelme

INTERVIEWED BY JEROME KLINKOWITZ

Donald Barthelme once said that Joyce's *Finnegans Wake* should be taken as part of the landscape, around which the reader's life could be slowly appreciated, like one's home or neighborhood. The weekly *New Yorker* with its Barthelme fiction, on the coffee table or next to the easy chair, provides a similar landscape for the appreciation of ongoing American fiction.

The author of four story collections, the novel *Snow White*, and the National Book Award winner for children's literature, *The Slightly Irregular Fire Engine*, Barthelme is one of the most prolific story writers in recent times: of his one-hundred-odd pieces, more than half have not been collected, among them some of his funniest and most inventive fictions. Barthelme's work has become one of the great resources of contemporary American literature; he has, according to Philip Stevick, become "the most imitated fictionist in the United States today." Like waiting for the next Charlie Parker single of a generation or two ago, avid Barthelme readers have a consistent and progressive stream of Barthelme to anticipate and collect. When *The New Yorker* is a day late and the girl across the hall has your paperbacks of *Come Back, Dr. Caligari; Unspeak-*

able Practices, Unnatural Acts; City Life; and *Sadness*, you can always boogie on down to the library and with the *Reader's Guide* spend a solid afternoon reading the uncollected Barthelme.

Though he declined a personal or telephone interview because of his "paranoia in the face of microphones," Barthelme accepted a list of questions mailed to his West 11th Street apartment in the fall of 1971. We kept in touch by phone thereafter; more questions were sent the next summer, from which the following twenty evolved. The first was suggested by fellow fictionist Carl Krampf, and the last was posed by Barthelme himself.

JEROME KLINKOWITZ: When you improvise, do you think of the chord changes or the melody?

DONALD BARTHELME: Both. This is an interesting question which I'm unable to answer adequately. If the melody is the skeleton of the particular object, then the chord changes are its wardrobe, its changes of clothes. I tend to pay rather more attention to the latter than to the former. All I want is just a trace of skeleton—three bones from which the rest may be reasoned out.

KLINKOWITZ: As the son of an architect, are you conscious of any influences of that art and science on your own fictional work? "At the Tolstoy Museum" and "The Show" feature architectural drawings, but I wonder if it has had a broader influence?

BARTHELME: My father was a "modern" architect in the sense that he was an advocate of Mies and Corbu, et al. He was something of an anomaly in Texas in the thirties. The atmosphere of the house was peculiar in that there were very large architectural books around and the considerations were: What was Mies doing, what was Aalto doing, what was Neutra up to, what about Wright? My father's concerns, in other words, were to say the least somewhat different from those of the other people we knew. His mind was elsewhere. My mother had a degree in English from Penn, where they had met, and was a Northerner, a Philadelphian. There were five children. In the late thirties my father built a house for us, something not too dissimilar to Mies's Tugendhat house. It was wonderful to live in but strange to see on the Texas prairie. On Sundays people used to park their cars out on the street and stare. We had a routine, the family, on Sundays. We used to get up from Sunday dinner, if enough cars had parked, and run out in front of the house in a sort of chorus line, doing high kicks.

The backgrounds in the "Tolstoy" and "Show" pieces are not architectural drawings but early (1603) investigations of perspective.

KLINKOWITZ: In a story you mention that you once "wrote poppycock for the president of a university." I imagine this was about the same time you were editing the University of Houston *Forum*. Did any experiences from those days, or when you edited *Location*, have influences on your fictional form, style, or subject matter? Can you tell me some of the things you did with these journals?

BARTHELME: First remember that the "I" of the story is not necessarily the author. Then let me admit that I did, in fact, while working for the university, write some speeches for the then president. Editing the quarterly at the university and later working for Tom Hess and Harold Rosenberg on *Location* in New York were both happy experiences. I had to look around quite a bit for material and thus read quite a number of things I wouldn't have otherwise, not only fiction but also pieces in the fields of philosophy, psychology, anthropology, history. I read all the learned journals for a while. I first encountered Walker Percy in (I believe) the *Journal of Philosophy and Phenomenological Research*. We printed two or three speculative pieces of his before I ever knew he wrote fiction. Then he sent us part of *The Moviegoer* and we (with great joy) printed that. I first encountered William Gass's work in the *Journal of Philosophy*. Again, I didn't know at that time that he wrote fiction. Similarly, we ran in *Forum* pieces by people like Joseph Lyons, Roger Callois, Robbe-Grillet, Sartre, Hugh Kenner, Gregory Bateson, Leslie Fiedler. Some strange and beautiful pieces. Later with *Location* we did more or less the same kind of thing, only with much more emphasis on art. We ran pieces by Bellow, McLuhan (this was before he got so famous), Gass, Koch, Ashbery,

etc. I enjoy editing and enjoy doing layout—problems of design. I
could very cheerfully be a typographer.

KLINKOWITZ: Are academics still of interest to you as they must
have been during the *Forum* period?

BARTHELME: Of course. But I'm not now reading the journals
as I did then. George Steiner is interesting, Ernst Bloch is interesting, etc. But I read their work in books, mostly (in the case of
Steiner, very often in the *New Yorker*). Probably I'm missing a
great deal. There is a need for a cross-disciplinary journal that
might provide a sampling of all the rest. Well-edited, such a journal
could be very valuable. *Intellectual Digest* is not it.

KLINKOWITZ: Some of your earliest stories published in the *New
Yorker* (and never collected) appear to be extended parodies of
language and the forms it takes when used by newswriters ("Snap,
Snap"), Italian directors ("L'lapse"), *Consumer Reports* ("Down
the Line with the Annual"), and *TV Guide* ("Man's Face: A New
Novel in Forty Coaxial Chapters"). Are such interests indeed the
wellsprings of your art?

BARTHELME: These pieces were not stories but more or less standard *New Yorker* parodies. I enjoyed writing them because I've
always admired the form at its best (for example, E. B. White's
beautiful "Dusk in Fierce Pajamas"). Wellsprings, no.

KLINKOWITZ: Aside from the security and rewards of such a good
market, is there any reason why you publish almost exclusively in
the *New Yorker*? John Updike and John Cheever built their careers
through such publication—do you have any sense that your own
pieces are catching a new style of our society and becoming latter-
day "*New Yorker*" stories, as Updike's and Cheever's may have
been for the decade before?

BARTHELME: Where else? I don't think there are, now, "*New
Yorker* stories." Not with Borges and Singer and Nabokov and
younger people like John Batki, as well as Updike and Cheever,
publishing there. These people are all very different, as you know.
And I trust the editors, especially Roger Angell, with whom I've

worked for about ten years now, who has saved me from many a horrendous error.

KLINKOWITZ: Are there any consistent or coherent themes that you intend for your series of short stories? Of late, "Perpetua" and "Critique de la Vie Quotidienne" seem to suggest this.

BARTHELME: No. "Perpetua" and the other story were both once parts of a novel which failed. As were "Henrietta and Alexandra" and "Flying to America." They may be thought of as the neck, wings, and drumsticks of a turkey. ("Flying to America" has been twice cannibalized, since I have drastically cut it and combined it with another story to make "A Film.")

KLINKOWITZ: In addition to all the incredible things you write about, such as a balloon expanding "northward all one night" from Fourteenth Street to Central Park or "thousands and thousands of porcupines" descending upon a university, you often feature quite realistic—even topically current—items in your stories, such as "And Now Let's Hear It for the Ed Sullivan Show!" and "Robert Kennedy Saved from Drowning," in which the events you describe actually happened. How do you see these and other aspects of our culture fitting into the general premises of your art? On the surface, it seems like a pretty big jump from the porcupines to Robert Kennedy.

BARTHELME: The Ed Sullivan piece was not a story but an assignment for *Esquire*. And nothing in the Robert Kennedy story actually happened except the bit in which Kennedy comments adversely on the work of a geometric painter. I was in that particular gallery on a day when Kennedy came in and made the comment reported. The rest of the story is, like, made up. It's not that aspects of the culture "fit into" any premise of mine, rather that the work is to this or that degree shaped by the culture.

KLINKOWITZ: Do you have any theories about "the novel"—its life, death, or whatever? So many innovative writers have talked about it: John Barth in "The Literature of Exhaustion"; Jerzy Kosinski, who fears that television has killed off its readers; and

Ronald Sukenick, who titled his novella "The Death of the Novel" and theorized about it as he wrote on. Any ideas?

BARTHELME: I think fewer people are reading. This has something to do with television and much to do, I think, with the fact that publishers are flooding the market with junk novels by what's-his-name and you-know-who and likewise—never mind. These odd productions make a lot of money, take up space both in the bookstores and in the minds of the readers, and effectively obscure the literary work. Gresham's Law. The situation does not, by the way, obtain in Europe, although the Europeans are learning. The question is, who is exhausted? Or what is exhausted? I invite you to notice that the new opium of the people is opium, or at least morphine. In a situation in which morphine contends with morpheme, the latter loses every time. There is also the problem of the allocation of the reader's time. To borrow a feather from Jules Renard—no matter how much care the writer has taken to write as few books as possible, there will still be people who don't know some of them.

KLINKOWITZ: What do you suppose are some of the new directions in fiction?

BARTHELME: The newest direction I've been able to perceive, given my American lack-of-languages, is John Ashbery's *Three Poems*, published this year (1972). These are three long prose pieces, quite amazing things. The German writer Jurgen Becker is doing something of the same sort, particularly in *Margins*, not yet published here except in excerpts. The German writer Peter Handke has opened some doors, for example in his sort-of-play *Self-Accusation*. The Viennese Oswald Wiener has written a half-novel, half-encyclopedia called *The Improvement of Central Europe: A Novel* (or something like that)—what I have seen of it suggests a new direction. We are having part of it translated for our newspaper, *Fiction*. In general the Germans seem to me more innovative, fresher, than the French at the moment.

KLINKOWITZ: Do you have any consciously formed notions about time and space that influence your work? Perception and imagination? Or, forgive me, "reality"?

BARTHELME: No.

KLINKOWITZ: In *Slaughterhouse-Five* Kurt Vonnegut, Jr., describes the Tralfamadorian "novel": " 'each clump of symbols is a brief, urgent message—describing a situation, a scene. We Tralfamadorians read them all at once, not one after the other. There isn't any particular relationship between all the messages, except that the author has chosen them carefully, so that, when seen all at once, they produce an image of life that is beautiful and surprising and deep. There is no beginning, no middle, no end, no suspense, no moral, no causes, no effects. What we love in our books are the depths of many marvelous moments seen all at one time' " (p. 76). That sounds like a Donald Barthelme novel, or story, to me. What do you think?

BARTHELME: I wish I could write something that would adequately satisfy Kurt's definition. Kenneth Koch's as yet unpublished novel *The Red Robins* may be it. John Ashbery's wonderful *Three Poems*, although not a novel, may be it.

KLINKOWITZ: Do you have plans for, or are you working on, another novel? *Snow White* seemed to me a logical extension, both thematically and structurally, of your short story craft. Are there any different directions you would want to explore in a new novel?

BARTHELME: I am always working on a novel. But they always seem to fall apart in my hands. I still have hopes, however.

KLINKOWITZ: In Richard Schickel's *New York Times Magazine* piece last year, you were reported as saying that "The principle of collage is the central principle of all art in the twentieth century in all media." Would you care to expand and perhaps tell me how it specifically applies to fiction?

BARTHELME: I was probably wrong, or too general. I point out however that New York City is or can be regarded as a collage, as opposed to, say, a tribal village in which all of the huts (or yurts, or whatever) are the same hut, duplicated. The point of collage is that unlike things are stuck together to make, in the best case, a new reality. This new reality, in the best case, may be or imply a comment on the other reality from which it came, and may be also much else. It's an *itself*, if it's successful: Harold Rosenberg's "anxious object," which does not know whether it's a work of art or a pile of junk. (Maybe I should have said that anxiety is the central principal of all art in the etc., etc.?)

KLINKOWITZ: Schickel also reported that you are "easily bored" and in fact "fear boredom." Is this simply a personal idiosyncrasy, or do you think it reflects a larger truth about the role of fiction— maybe all art—in our times?

BARTHELME: I doubt that this is a condition peculiar to me. For example, I have trouble reading, in these days. I would rather drink, talk, or listen to music. The difficulties the painters are now having —the problem of keeping *themselves* interested—are I think instructive. Earthworks, conceptual art, etc., seem to me last resorts. Now there is a certain virtue in finding the absolutely last resort— being the Columbus of the last resort—but I don't think I'd enjoy the role. I do a lot of failing and that keeps me interested.

KLINKOWITZ: Are there any immediate popular sources for or influences on your art—TV, comic books, rock music, jazz? Or is there a common popular sensibility you might be aware of? Or any deeper cultural sources?

BARTHELME: As a raw youth, I was very interested in jazz. Similarly I now listen to rock constantly. In writing I pay a great deal of attention to rhythm, but I suppose everyone else does too. I'm very interested in awkwardness: sentences that are awkward in a particular way. As to "deeper cultural sources," I have taken a certain degree of nourishment (or stolen a lot) from the phenomenologists: Sartre, Erwin Straus, etc.

KLINKOWITZ: Do you have any favorite comedians, and reasons for liking them?

BARTHELME: The government.

KLINKOWITZ: Can you tell me about any of your favorite writers and reasons for liking them? Or artists in other media?

BARTHELME: Among writers of the past, I'd list Rabelais, Rimbaud, Kleist, Kafka, Stein, and Flann O'Brien.

Among living writers, Beckett, Gass, Percy, Marquez, Barth, Pynchon, Kenneth Koch, John Ashbery, Grace Paley.

Artists in other media: too many.

KLINKOWITZ: Did growing up in Texas warp you in any particular way? I only ask this because so many writers from Texas have proclaimed themselves Texas writers (whereas I have heard of few New Jersey writers). Or were you simply "born in Philadelphia" —and leave it at that?

BARTHELME: I don't think I'm a Texas writer in the sense that, say, Larry McMurtry is. I don't write about Texas. And "warp" I wouldn't say. I learned to read the signs of the dominant culture well enough, learned to impersonate a Texan well enough. It gave me something to place the rest of the world over against, as the philosophers say. That is, I could enjoy the difference. That I've lived in New York for the last ten years (except for a year in Europe) does not mean that I don't also enjoy Texas. I left with pleasure and return with pleasure.

KLINKOWITZ: In your story "See the Moon" one of the characters has the line, "Fragments are the only forms I trust." This has been quoted as a statement of your aesthetic. Is it?

BARTHELME: No. It's a statement by the character about what he is feeling at that particular moment. I hope that whatever I think about aesthetics would be a shade more complicated than that. Because that particular line has been richly misunderstood so often (most recently by my colleague J. C. Oates in the *Times*) I have thought of making a public recantation. I can see the story in, say, *Women's Wear Daily*:

WRITER CONFESSES
THAT HE NO LONGER
TRUSTS FRAGMENTS

TRUST 'MISPLACED,'
AUTHOR DECLARES

DISCUSSED DECISION
WITH DAUGHTER, SIX

WILL SEEK 'WHOLES'
IN FUTURE, HE SAYS

CLOSING TIME IN
GARDENS OF WEST
WILL BE EXTENDED,
SCRIVENER STATES

New York, June 24 (A&P)—
Donald Barthelme, 41-year-old
writer and well-known fragma-
tist, said today that he no longer
trusted fragments. He added
that although he had once been
"very fond" of fragments, he
had found them to be "finally
untrustworthy."

The author, looking tense and
drawn after what was described
as "considerable thought," made
his dramatic late-night an-
nouncement at a Sixth Avenue
laundromat press conference,
from which the press was
excluded.

Sources close to the soap
machine said, however, that the
agonizing reappraisal, which
took place before their eyes,
required only four minutes.

"Fragments fall apart a lot,"
Barthelme said. Use of antelope
blood as a bonding agent had
not proved . . . .

Ronald Sukenick

INTERVIEWED BY JOE DAVID BELLAMY

Up, Ronald Sukenick's first full-length fictional work, was published by Dial in 1968 to enthusiastic reviews. The "novel" was "a hilarious outburst of wild comedy," according to *Saturday Review*; "an action painting in words," according to the *New York Times*. In 1969 Sukenick followed with *The Death of the Novel and Other Stories*, an effort through total improvisation, tape recording, and collage, "to get fiction back to the truth of experience," according to the description on the dust jacket.

Sukenick's second novel, *Out*, published in 1973 by Swallow, is a daring formal experiment described as "an effort to get back to a blank page from which we can start over again." Sukenick's fiction has also appeared in numerous magazines: *New American Review, Partisan Review, Paris Review, fiction international*, and others.

The Sukenicks and Domino, an enormous, aged Dalmatian, arrived at the Cornell University English Department to meet me in midafternoon on August 13, 1970. While waiting for Sukenick's classes to begin, we sat in the *Epoch* office, which doubles as a classroom, and tried to decide if the classes would be worth taping. Lynn (Sukenick's wife) and the dog drifted out. The next hours were spent in classes—the first a creative writing class and the second a class in the modern novel, which happened on that day to be discussing Henry Miller's *Tropic of Capricorn*.

The following interview took place on the evening of August 13, 1970, and on into the morning of August 14, at Sukenick's temporary summer home, a French Provincial mansion in Ithaca, New York.

JOE DAVID BELLAMY: Shortly after the appearance of your first novel, *Up*, a review in *Newsweek* described you as one of a "new constellation" of younger writers who showed promise of starting something of significance, of "working unmined land." The one characteristic that the *Newsweek* review pointed out which seemed to link you with the other writers mentioned was your concern for fantasy. You seem to take fantasy very seriously, which writers haven't done so much before, until recently it seems. And yet in certain respects this seems to be an emphasis on the kinds of things which literature has always been concerned about, one of which is—illusion.

RONALD SUKENICK: Well, how can I put this?—one of the reasons people have lost faith in the novel is that they don't believe it tells the truth anymore, which is another way of saying that they don't believe in the convention of the novel. They pick up a novel and they know it's make-believe. So, who needs it—go listen to the television news, right? Or read a biography. Okay, if you could forget that business about illusion, you'd be more honest. Nobody is willing to suspend disbelief in that particular way anymore, including me. So once you get to the point where you admit that you are writing a book and it *is* a book, there really is no difference between fantasy and realistic action. It's completely continuous—it's all made up.

BELLAMY: You mean it's all part of experience?

SUKENICK: I mean *on the page* it's obviously all made up; it's no different. Here I am a writer writing on a blank page, and there's really no division between if I write a dream and if I write what happened yesterday—it's all what I'm writing. To put it one way, it's all make-believe. To put it another way, it's all the real act of writing, which is not make-believe but is a real act of the imagination.

BELLAMY: Do you think of the novel as a set form—as this kind of thing that's already happened in history and not as a thing that's progressing and changing all the time?

SUKENICK: Well, I think that the kind of imaginative act that goes into a novel, let's say fiction, is so basic to human consciousness that it antedates the novel, and the novel is a particular form of it. And it will change after the novel, and probably we'll go on calling things the novel because, you know, we call things novels now that one couldn't possibly imagine as novels in 1910.

But there seems to be movement. For example, one direction seems to be the direction of myth; people seem to be constructing myths; like, Coover seems to be interested in myths, say, and Joyce obviously. I'm not interested in that, but that's one direction.

It's a question of breaking down the conventions of realism. It's just that the novel has been identified with realism for so long, you know, so when you say the novel you think of the realistic novel. To say that the novel is dead is silly—even though I called one of my books *The Death of the Novel and Other Stories*. The *"Other Stories"* means I think that's silly, really. It's just that the novel is moving into new forms.

Another direction is biography and autobiography—like the whole rash of guys who are writing, at very young ages, their autobiographies, which seems to be a substitute for writing a novel. Ah, but that's tricky though, because something like *Stop-Time*, for example—you know, that, in an odd way, seems more like a conventional novel than an autobiography. That is, you know—without putting it down—it's, you know, it's all right; but it's as if one is reading a slightly disorganized *Bildungsroman*. But what I mean is that he doesn't seem to be taking full advantage of the autobiographical form. It seems like autobiography influenced by the Victorian novel. And you could almost as well be reading a novel except that it's called, and it is, an autobiography. But his imagination seems to cast itself more or less in the form of a novel.

BELLAMY: I wonder what the form of the autobiography is, if there really is any kind of hard and fast form especially suited to autobiography?

SUKENICK: Well, there isn't. Probably, in the past, autobiography was always dictated by other forms around. So, you know, it's a question of how you imagine the shape of your life; I don't see my life in terms of sequential events, in terms of progress. So I don't see my life in terms of plot, or of an advance. If I were to write an autobiography, which *Up* isn't but resembles in some ways, I guess, it probably wouldn't be sequential at all, but patched together. I guess a good example of that is Genet, who clearly uses autobiography but uses it to synthesize a new form. He doesn't really care about his past. What he's interested in is defining his present and constructing a character. And that seems to be a vast departure from the sense of recounting of a past that you get in a *Bildungsroman*.

BELLAMY: Uh-huh.

SUKENICK: But actually I really do think that it's probably a healthy act to say that the novel is dead—if only that it enables you to forget about it and to start thinking about new forms. Because I don't really think that novels should come out of a tradition of the novel. I think they should come out of your own experience—especially now when our present seems very discontinuous from a recent past. It seems to be all the more important that you should get rid of old forms and allow new forms to grow out of your own experience. It seems to me that the novel form is a block, that there are all these talented people around trying to write in this form which doesn't suit them at all, so that instead of releasing their energies it blocks them out.

BELLAMY: Would you say that you are adhering to some kind of idea of progress in literature, that is, that literature must, of necessity, change and progress?

SUKENICK: I guess there are things called traditions in which people are influenced by their predecessors. But I think that tends to be overestimated by academic estimates of how things occur. I think that healthy literature, live literature, is more influenced by what's going on in the present and that people use what they know of past literature just the way they use what they know of past history, say, or philosophy.

BELLAMY: Would you say that literature which is contemporary is somehow "better" than previous great literature or simply equal to the best of other times?

SUKENICK: Well, no, I don't think it's better. . . . I love Jane Austen, for example, and George Eliot, but they don't help me very much, personally—I mean both in writing and in life. So it's the difference between going to a museum and going to a contemporary exhibit.

BELLAMY: Isn't there probably an element of marketability about the idea of the death of the novel? That is, there are a lot of people who are very committed to fiction, whether it be the novel or some other form, and all this talk about the death of the novel is a very scary sort of thing to these people. They usually tend to extend it into fiction in general. That is, maybe fiction really is dying—there are no more markets for it and things like that—symptoms. And you seem to sort of even have that idea maybe in the title of your book *The Death of the Novel*. It seems clear that if people are afraid of the death of the novel, they will buy a book which has the "death of the novel" in its title. Or they will read critical essays on the "death of the novel" for fear that something they place great value in really is dying.

SUKENICK: Well, I think it *is* dying—I mean, in a familiar form. I don't think that people trust novels anymore. I don't think that students go to novels now in the same way that they used to in the fifties—with the sense that they were going to learn something about their lives, the way that people used to read Hemingway, say. I think that in its realistic forms it's just lost its credibility. And maybe that is what I mean, or what one means, when one says "the death of the novel." People don't believe that it tells the truth about anything. People are surrounded by all sorts of information coming in to them through all sorts of media now, and the novel, on that level, doesn't have anything to say to them. They know that they can get the same kind of thing out of a television broadcast and the news or something like that.

BELLAMY: Another thing that seems to interest you is the writing process itself. You don't efface yourself as an author, obviously; you talk about the writing process quite a lot; for example, in "The Death of the Novel," where you continually say "I can't go on . . . Go on," which always does go on in the typical kind of writer's experience—and in "What's Your Story," I think, it is the striking out of things and changing them.

SUKENICK: Yeah, "I can't go on . . . Go on" is a sort of Beckett echo. Beckett was influencing me at one point, and I think it's *Malone Dies* where he's writing along like that and it's boring and he's saying "I can't go on." But for me it's a way of getting into the flow of life and out of the form of the novel.

BELLAMY: So you don't believe in any of the old Jamesian buga-boos about the need to efface yourself.

SUKENICK: Oh absolutely not, no. I mean, that's, of course, what I was brought up with and, you know, hung over me, a tremendous weight—and then I really had to escape.

BELLAMY: It seems to me that you've proved that it was a pretty bad theory to start with, just as I believe Wayne Booth in *The Rhetoric of Fiction* explodes many of the old clichés about fiction criticism by showing that James himself was committing some of these sins and others—and other great novelists as well were doing such things.

SUKENICK: Well, it was good for James, you know. James was a great writer, you know. I really like James; it suited his particular personality. The trouble was that for a long time it became a whole theory of writing for everybody. You know, I think that writing styles are very personal things, and it's a mistake to make theories of writing, really. My theories of writing are for two things: mainly, they're to release me into my writing, but also, I suppose, there is a propaganda side. I want people to get off one kind of book and get onto another kind of book which seems to me more appropriate for what's going on now—to get people unstuck from a formulated kind of response and open them up to another thing.

BELLAMY: Getting back to the subject of fantasy, in your work in general there is a sense that the fantasies you're having are fantasies you would have anyway; that is, you're not making them up for the purpose of entertaining someone. . . .

SUKENICK: Oh, yeah, that's true. I'll put it this way: they're not fantasies I would have anyway; they're fantasies I'm having at the moment of writing.

BELLAMY: So, looking at it from a conventional perspective, in a way that fiction has been talked about before, it's all part of your revelation of character—so that a character is dramatized more fully because his fantasies are related.

SUKENICK: What's happening actually is that I'm *making up* my character. I mean, I'm really a very amorphous individual, as a matter of fact. That's a true admission—that I'm an amorphous individual. And what happens when I write is that I'm making myself up. Maybe if I become a more hardened type, more of a character, that need will disappear. But actually what I feel I'm working toward is that thing I was saying about Miller in class. I really believe that we have an enormous need to dissolve our character structures; so probably that business will continue for me.

BELLAMY: Taking on a character is doing that as well though, isn't it—taking on or identifying with one of the characters you write—as well as defining your own character by dramatizing it?

SUKENICK: I don't understand that.

BELLAMY: I mean, one thing that was said of Faulkner—and it is often said of writers—is that Faulkner apparently enjoyed sort of getting inside all these different people, either as an escape from his own personality or for whatever reason—making himself up. For example, he had this costume which was a hunting costume with a red coat, with a top hat which he wore sometimes. . . .

SUKENICK: I see what you're getting at. I'm not like that. I have no sense of the dramatic in that way.

BELLAMY: On paper though, would you say you do?

SUKENICK: No, it doesn't work that way for me. I absolutely don't have a feeling that, say, take the character Otis in *Up*—I don't have the feeling that I'm inside Otis and that he's an extension of my personality. I have a similar feeling. I have a feeling that he represents a segment of my personality. You know, like, if the mind is a stage, he's one of the actors; and there are other actors. What happens at the end of *Up* is that all the characters collapse, and it turns out that they're all inside my head. And then we go out to real characters in the real world.

So, it may be the equivalent of the kind of thing you're talking about. I don't feel as if I project myself into a character at all, but I feel that insofar as I have characters (which isn't too much because those people in that book are sort of comic characters or caricatures anyway), I feel they're sort of dialectical divisions of my own personality, this trend and that trend. But that's only half of it. The other half of it is that, in any case, I feel that the imagination is a faculty of perception. It's not an extra faculty, but a faculty that's essential, that one uses all the time. Otherwise you couldn't get along from one moment to the next. I mean, you're always making people up, in effect. I mean, like, there you are, and I don't know much about you, but, in a way, I'm making you up. I'm filling up the gaps in my mind, and I create the Joe Bellamy that happens to be there. And probably there's a great gap between my version, which is imaginative, and the real Joe Bellamy.

BELLAMY: What *is* the real Joe Bellamy though?

SUKENICK: Well, I don't know. I was going to say maybe there isn't a real Joe Bellamy. Maybe there aren't real characters. That's an important thing. Maybe people are much more fluid and amorphous than the realistic novel would have us believe.

BELLAMY: That's probably true, but I'm thinking: In a way, don't we all make ourselves up—even if we don't write? Even if....

SUKENICK: Oh, yes, of course. I just think what I'm doing in that respect is an imitation of how we perceive things.

BELLAMY: That gets into all sorts of questions like how good an actor one becomes in acting out what one is making one's self to be. That seems to make it somehow artificial.

SUKENICK: Well, I don't know what you mean. There's an act of will involved? Well, sometimes there is, in different cases. Genet clearly, as he comes through in his books, is an artifice—and sheer artifice. First of all, there's the sense in which a homosexual has made up his own character anyway because it involves a denial of masculinity—for some homosexuals. It seems to for Genet. That particular type of homosexual is then proceeding on the basis of artifice, very clearly. Now I think one reason why Genet is important is that in his case it's an extreme transition. It simply makes clear what we all do, you see what I mean? It's especially clear in the case of a transvestite homosexual, a queen. I think that, in fact, we have a certain amout of data about ourselves that we know about, and we organize it in this way or that way according to this or that ego structure. And then, in fact, people's sense of themselves shifts according to situations that they find themselves in, and even more drastically according to traumatic experiences they might pass through in their lives.

BELLAMY: Most people suffer from a limited imagination in regard to what they are. They believe what people have told them about their limitations or whatever.

SUKENICK: Right, that kind of thing that Genet does is enormously liberating. Because if you see what he's doing, then it allows you the liberty to then go on to realize that you are amorphous; you're just a locus of consciousness and operating possibly on one possible ego structure. And when you see that there are all sorts of possibilities. . . . But there's something wrong with that. What's wrong is the element of will. I mean, I don't think the imagination has to be that perverse, especially by yourself.

BELLAMY: Why do you say perverse?

SUKENICK: Well, I mean, it's perverse in the sense that to perform an act of will to create an identity seems to get away from some essential given—maybe—if there are such things as givens. I mean,

I can follow the Genet route so far, and then I sense that there's an area of aesthetics and playacting that I don't want to get into. Because I *do* feel after all that there may not be an absolute Sukenick, but there are some givens. . . . Well, one of the things is—character structure hides deeper levels. I mean, character structure is a choice that eliminates certain things that come from your, say, subconscious or unconscious and selects others. Now, for me, the liberating thing is to choose not from the social or from some catalog but to allow all the possibilities in your personality. So, I guess I do think that there are things that are there to be released.

But the kind of character structure that you find in a Victorian novel, say, or as I was talking about, the hardened characters, characters in a colloquial sense, or hard character structure of the kind that a Victorian businessman had to be to get through life, or almost anybody in that period had to be to get through life, is very limiting and ought to be dissolved in the direction of greater possibility.

Someday I hope to be able to face all the possibilities in my own personality and come to some kind of agreement with them and then live with them, but in the meantime my drive is to dissolve character. I think that that's not only a need on my part, but I presume to think that that's also a cultural need for a lot of people, for the culture in general perhaps. And I think that it is *happening* that modes of character are breaking down, as a matter of fact. They're becoming inadequate.

BELLAMY: *Can* you get rid of your own ego . . . ?

SUKENICK: Ego structure, character. . . .

BELLAMY: So that you become this focus of consciousness rather than this person with a name who has a certain status in society and certain attitudes?

SUKENICK: Yeah, and allow wider possibilities to arise in yourself. . . .

BELLAMY: Acting out different personalities, how can they ever rejoin, then? That's what I mean. You said that sometime they'll all be resolved into one.

SUKENICK: Maybe what happens finally is that you open an awareness into multiple possibilities and multiple levels of personality, and you can be an infinite number of beings: at one point a mature businessman and at another point a vulnerable infant—when you're making love or something like that—or a certain point in making love—and a mature businessman, acting aggressively and in a very defined way when you have to. But at either point you're aware and conscious of the other possibility, and it's not lost but just put aside for a while.

BELLAMY: But isn't that true now?

SUKENICK: Well, . . . my sense of things is that—I think students get very excited over drugs precisely because it releases a highly strictured and structured character that they've developed, that they've grown up with, and opens them out into different areas of themselves. I think this is reflected in a whole literary trend. I don't think the kinds of books I'm interested in are interested in characterization anymore. In Kafka you get K. In *Finnegans Wake* you get characters who are totally fluid. One person becomes another person. H. C. E. becomes Persse O'Reilly or this or that. People are constantly changing persona within a limited range. There's the father figure or the king figure, and anything that fits into that is H. C. E., and it keeps changing. And it's not only a personality change, it's a time change. With Joyce and with Kafka you get a cipher; you don't get a character. You get K. And in Beckett you sometimes get somebody who's a locus who not only doesn't know who he is, he doesn't know what he is—I guess that's the extreme—and in Miller you get the whole process. You get somebody who is consciously trying to destroy his own character.

I got very excited recently reading Reich—Wilhelm, that is—who I'd read a long time ago and who had influenced me a lot a long time ago in a different way because I didn't understand it in the same way. I got very excited. I was thinking along this kind of line and also thinking about the same kind of thing in myself. This is not a literary matter for me. I just happened to see it reflected in certain books. But I rediscovered that that's what Reich

is trying to do. The idea of Reichian analysis is to dissolve character
—finally to dissolve bad character structure and allow other or-
ganizations to arise. When you get that kind of thing, it seems you
feel it in yourself, you see it all around you; you see it in the books
you like, and you see it in the psychoanalytic writings you like,
and you get very excited about it, and you get the feeling that
maybe you're on the right track.

One of the things that interests me is what to do with the concept
of characterization. And I guess—well, I don't know what I'm
going to do with it—but one of the things I did in "The Birds"
was to purposely make characters with characteristics that absolutely didn't go together, whose names serve as rubrics for totally disparate traits. You get a character with some name, say Sparrow;
and at one point he's described as short and at another he's
described as tall. Or, there's a whole episode like that in the novel-
ette in *The Death of the Novel*, one of those little bits, one of those
little stories within a story where the guy is describing his landlord
or some guy he thinks might be his landlord. First he describes
him as little and then he describes him as big, and then he says
he can't remember what he looks like at all.

BELLAMY: Another aspect of this—in reading "What's Your
Story," I went along thinking, "This is realistic or autobiographical,
one of the two." But about halfway through I started questioning
that, so that toward the end I decided they really *were* fantasy
characters I was reading about. So, it seems that you proceed from
this complete suspension of disbelief, which I was willing to do, and
these characters who I believed either really were characters in
your life—or you had made them realistic enough that I really
believed them—and then you allowed them to be fantasies or
admitted they were fantasies. Although I still wasn't sure, I wondered if you weren't concealing the fact; I wondered if you hadn't
decided to act as if they were fantasy characters to conceal the fact
that they were autobiographical.

SUKENICK: In "What's your Story" I made them more . . . fantasy
characters—they're all characters from old stories—although I sort

of made them more fantastic at the end, hoping to make it clear that they were fantasy characters. Although I really didn't hope that people would realize it, some people did. In an odd way that's the most autobiographical story in the book. All the locations are real locations; all the desks are real desks; and I talk about how stories occur to me while I'm sitting at the desks and trying to reproduce how those old stories actually occurred to me. I think in the first one there's a girl who's there sleeping with me, and I start talking about her and I develop her in the way that, in fact, I developed her in a story, my first published story. See, what they are—they're characters from different old stories coming together in one story and saying "hello."

BELLAMY: Another idea I started thinking about—one more or less obscure function that fiction might serve, if it has any cultural function or psychological function, is to press for both the writer and the reader to concern themselves with taboo subjects. I guess in one way that's what fantasy really is. . . .

SUKENICK: What are taboo subjects now?

BELLAMY: Well, that's true. Nothing in fiction. But I mean in comparison to what people do in life, what ordinary people do in life. Fiction becomes this way of behaving as you might wish to behave if your id was a little freer, but really aren't able to, and so fiction becomes this vehicle through which you express your id wishes.

SUKENICK: It's not that way for me. But the thing is, in *Up* it's a confusing situation. I'm sure it's confusing for readers who care about this kind of thing. I mean, people who we knew peripherally would call up after the book was published and say who was this and who was that and was that so-and-so? And it wasn't like that at all because there are no real characters in it except in the end when I put in real characters. I mean, *those* are real characters— those are my friends. But the people who are in there before that are really imaginary characters, and they do bear a certain relation to my experience. The incidents do bear a certain relation to my experience. And there's no telling which is which. I mean, there's no telling for the reader, and in a way, above all, after a while there's no telling for me. Some of the things in there you would think were not made up, were; and some of the things that you might think were made up, were not. The point is that there's no telling.

But the business about taboos *became* important for me at a certain point in writing because I realized that I was censoring myself. I mean, I think we, everybody, has his own personal taboos—anything goes in public—unless the Berger court makes it different. But I think it's actually very hard to escape personal taboos, because it's very hard to escape personal repression. And I suddenly, at one point, had the overwhelming realization that I was just—you know. . . . Well, the way it happened was this: I did a double take—because I started thinking of writing something, and then I had a reaction that was almost subconscious which went: I can't write that. But for some reason it was just conscious enough for me to catch it, and I suddenly realized the extent to which I was censoring myself. What happened was I caught myself just on the verge of forgetting the whole episode. It went like this: idea to write something, I can't write that, forget it! And in another second it would have been obliterated. For some reason I caught it and realized the degree that I was canceling things out. That was a very important moment for me, crucial maybe.

BELLAMY: So you decided to stop doing that?

SUKENICK: As much as you can, yeah. It's hard to stop doing that, but as much as I could.

BELLAMY: One impulse you've suggested consistently, and an aspect that I would say characterizes your work, *is* what one might call frankness. I don't know if that's an apt word. But I think of it as honesty, you know, willingness to keep the censor at bay.

SUKENICK: I think that is something important.

BELLAMY: It is.

SUKENICK: There are, you know, those who say that sincerity isn't important in literature—because one of the things that students are always saying in beginning English classes is: "I like that because that's very sincere." Now, of course, that's a shallow response, but I think that's an honest response and an important response. And it shouldn't be blanked out; it should only be deepened and located. I think that fiction should tell the truth. I think that people should be honest in fiction, and I think that's absolutely one of the most important things about it. That doesn't mean that you have to write autobiography. One of the reasons that the novel is "dead" is that people just don't believe what the novel is saying anymore. And in most cases they're right.

BELLAMY: Still, the question of taboos. For example, I'm thinking in "Permanent Crisis"—the question comes up: maybe the narrator shouldn't have married his wife.

SUKENICK: Well, there was no taboo as far as I was concerned because I made up that story before I ever met my wife.

BELLAMY: But how many people, both husbands and wives in this world, have entertained the wish to have such a thought as that but immediately repress it? That is, it's a question you never ask because it's too threatening, perhaps, at least for the average person. And yet *you* ask it, and in that sense it becomes an articulation of this smoggy area of repressed material. (It's an honest kind of question that maybe people should ask—but that they refuse to ask.)

In "Momentum" one of the immediate items of interest is the fact that you mention Lynn as your wife. The reader may not know that Lynn is your real wife, but you mention, the narrator mentions, that he has this wife, and then he goes out with this girl during the visit. And there is no mention of the wife. There seems to be no kind of questioning for quite a ways, nothing about the inconsistency in this or any moral qualms at all and a very realistically callous attitude toward this girl, which is sort of delightful, unquestioning....

SUKENICK: That's funny—I always thought about that story that it wasn't callous enough about that girl.

BELLAMY: It seems to be what people might like to do if they could, only most of them can't—because they would get sentimentally attached to the girl or couldn't bring it off. They'd have moral qualms; they'd be in all kinds of cross-currents. But you managed to do it. So, again, it becomes this kind of articulation or living out of a wish which other people might like to live out but can't. Maybe taboo is a bad word for that. It is an articulation or a dramatization of something that people would like to do if they could, so it becomes a living out of a fantasy, in a sense.

SUKENICK: Ah . . . for the reader.

BELLAMY: Yeah.

SUKENICK: Ah.

BELLAMY: And also with Teddy, for example, in "The Death of the Novel"—I mean, how many older men would really love to make it with a fifteen-year-old cutie but never get a chance to or could never bring themselves to?

SUKENICK: But, on the other hand, that's been the subject of a lot of fiction in the last four or five years, five or six years. . . .

BELLAMY: Right, right, right, it's not new, but it still works. It's an enduring fantasy. You don't have to be the first one to have it.

SUKENICK: What I'm trying to say is that I don't think that's of particular value. Because you could probably get that situation, that story, told in comic strips by now, or maybe in movies anyway, and it's been the subject of a lot of fiction; so, as I say, I don't consider it of particular value.

BELLAMY: One might argue that the real measure of a successful novelist is his ability to parcel out generally held fantasies of the population—so that people can participate in these fantasies without feeling guilt. And I think I really could make a case for your fiction doing that—clear across the board.

SUKENICK: Maybe you could. I never thought of that.

BELLAMY: So your fantasies are everyone's fantasies—and that's one of the reasons for the success of your work, aside from a lot of other considerations.

SUKENICK: Could you elaborate on that a little?

BELLAMY: Well, one explanation I've heard for the success of *Valley of the Dolls....*

SUKENICK: Of who?

BELLAMY: Jacqueline Susann's *Valley of the Dolls;* it's a horribly written book. Anyway, supposedly it's a reliving of the typical fantasy of the middle-aged woman on Main Street in the Midwest— or anywhere in America: this fantasy of going to New York and being a career girl. Only she's married; she's stuck in her own town. What eventually gets proven in *Valley of the Dolls* is that if you do go to New York—well, first of all, it *allows* you to *be* a career girl, *go* to New York, *have* affairs with interesting men, escape your humdrum existence—but you begin to see that this existence becomes more and more complicated. In fact, the people involved become suicidal and very depressed and finally in the end are either unhappy or commit suicide. So what it eventually proves to you is that you're really better off being back in wherever-you-are anyway. So it leaves you with this satisfying feeling. It allows you to have the fantasy but also to escape it. And that's the possible explanation for its success.

SUKENICK: Well, I immediately react adversely to that. I don't want to indulge people's fantasies. Maybe it's like the difference between Brechtian theatre and Aristotelian theatre. I don't want to present people with illusions, and I don't want to let them off cheaply by releasing their fantasies in an easy way. If the stuff has done that, okay. It's probably inevitable in any case, but it's not really the kind of thing I'm trying to do. I never thought about it very much; but if I ever did get around to really considering it, I would probably try to think of a way to prevent that from happen- ing, which is an interesting idea, as a matter of fact. Because what that does is allow people to escape, obviously, from reality, and I want to bang them with it.

BELLAMY: Wow.

SUKENICK: I want to force them to get back into. . . . What?

BELLAMY: What *is* fantasy— if it's not a part of reality? It seems to me that one thing that I enjoy about your work is its *relish* of fantasy, not as an escape but as a part of reality.

SUKENICK: Yeah, it's a part of reality insofar as you get people to admit their fantasies and dispel them or at least admit them and find out about them. That's one thing. But to allow them to indulge them is different, and that's something I don't want to do.

BELLAMY: Well, I don't see this as some kind of indulgence and escapism but as a kind of therapy.

SUKENICK: But that's purgative. I don't want people to purge themselves of their feelings about fantasy because that allows them to have their fantasy and forget it, and then when it comes up again they have it again. What I'd rather do is get people to recognize the nature of their fantasies.

BELLAMY: I guess I have implicit sort of Freudian statements about what the artist does. He had several different ones, but the one I'm thinking about is this idea that the artist is like a child—it's in "The Relation of the Poet To Daydreaming." Supposedly, as children, most people daydream, they relish their daydreams, they act out their daydreams. When they reach adulthood, they lose the capacity to act out their daydreams. The daydreams are various egotistical kinds of wishes, erotic wishes, and they find that these kinds of wishes, if expressed, are unacceptable. Their peers are put off by those kinds of wishes. That is, it's best to conceal those sorts of things, so people repress them and they become guilty about their daydreams. Freud said the artist is a person who is not guilty about his daydreams and who by various kinds of disguises is able to make his daydreams acceptable to all those people who don't find them acceptable—so that they are able to participate in them.

SUKENICK: Yeah, but the trouble is that that makes imagining a kind of safety valve, and I don't see it that way at all. I guess that's artistic sublimation, isn't it? I don't see it that way at all. For example, I'm not interested in dreams. Some of the things I've written about, some of the things I put in *Up*, for instance, come straight out of my dreams; and I'm not interested in those things. I don't want to use them as things to analyze. What I'm interested in them as is another level of reality, which we can make use of and include. Does that make any sense? Maybe not. Let's see if I can put it a different way. I had a dream, the scene in *Up* where there's a figure of a mummy wrapped up. That was a dream, and I got up and wrote it down, you know. I thought I'd put it in, but I discovered afterwards an obvious connection between mummy and "mummy," you know, mommy. But that's not what I had in mind —although if that's there it makes it all the more resonant. What I had in mind was to use it as another building block in the creation of the identity that was going on. I didn't care, for purposes of writing, I don't care, what the dream or fantasy material indicated about my hidden personality. I want to make use of that stuff if it's interesting. I wish I could make that clear.

BELLAMY: I think I know what you mean. But what I'm getting at with Freud's idea is—what Freud would have said is that this attempt that you have made, wanting people to come to the same realization that you have about fantasies, is futile. What you're trying to do is make everyone an artist and *you're* the artist. You have the realization that fantasies are good and don't need to be repressed, and in a sense society gives you the consent to indulge your fantasies as an artist; that's your role. If you were an average person you couldn't do that—because you'd be ridiculed; you'd be stoned perhaps; you'd be disliked.

SUKENICK: But that seems reductive. I mean, say you take the Oedipus play merely as wish fulfillment, an acting-out sort of thing. It seems really to reduce the value of the play enormously. Or, to put it another way, if you use Freud on Oedipus, what you get finally is Freud, not Oedipus.

BELLAMY: Right, what you're giving is the old argument against psychological criticism in general.

SUKENICK: I mean, I do believe—I read a writer like Genet or somebody equally obvious in personality structure, and I don't want to blank out any kind of psychological recognition there. But, on the other hand, Genet's writing, especially in *Our Lady of the*

Flowers, is totally masturbatory, totally a masturbation fantasy. But there's something much more than that as well, luckily. Because if it were only a masturbation fantasy, who would care? On top of which, a lot of homosexuals really wouldn't care because it really wouldn't have erotic effect. But he uses it, it seems to me, in a superior structure and transcends the initial fantasy meaning.

BELLAMY: I'm not trying to diminish the importance of a work as a literary or aesthetic achievement. I'm just trying to get at some of the possible psychological reasons why fiction exists.

SUKENICK: I think there are epistemological reasons before there are psychological reasons. After all, myth is a way of organizing the world that antecedes philosophy.

BELLAMY: Okay. I agree. That gets through everything, it seems to me.

SUKENICK: I mean, my whole idea about fiction is that it's a normal, if I may use the word, epistemological procedure; that is, it is at the very center of everybody all the time at any period, and you don't have to search for psychological reasons, although they may be there too. But I think the epistemological ones are far more important and anterior. It's a way of making up the world and making sense of it.

Tom Wolfe

INTERVIEWED BY JOE DAVID BELLAMY

"Well, hello there, Senator," quips the over-rouged lady in the air-terminal lobby. Obviously, she is referring to my friend in the Big Lunch tie, the slightly yellowing white suit, the blue suede shoes, the blue-and-white checkered shirt and socks, the one day's growth of light beard on his face, the copy of *Sporting News* rolled up under his arm, the nicely chiseled nose, and the Stetson. . . . Obviously, she has no idea who she is addressing. "Jesus, lady," I say to myself.

Hardly a mere senator, the man in the white suit is, in fact, Tom Wolfe. It is March in New York's "North Country," and that evening at 9:00 Tom Wolfe is presenting another lecture on "The New Journalism"—this time at St. Lawrence University. . . . If he takes any note of the offensive, over-rouged lady, his reaction is skillfully suppressed.

Later, out on the road, we discuss Balzac. "My great discovery of the last eighteen months," Wolfe says, "has been Balzac. I never read anything by him before that. . . ." He goes on to advocate a return to Balzacian principles as a solution to the problems of contemporary fiction writers. Why is it, I wonder, that "the most famous pop writer in America" worries about such problems? Why does he *really* go around lecturing on the "new journalism" and writing articles called "Why They Aren't Writing the Great American Novel Anymore"? What sort of phenomenon am I dealing with here, Jim?

Well, one little-known fact about Tom Wolfe helps put this in perspective: he is really Dr. Wolfe. That's right, Jim. Sorry to disillusion you. Terrible Tom, Tom the Wolfe-Man, *New York*'s clean-up hitter, *Esquire*'s boy; *Rolling Stone*'s latest head; Ken Kesey's buddy—he is really a Yale Ph.D. in disguise. Holy ———!

Another thing, Jim. Beneath the elegant flamboyance of his clothes, he is a sort of quiet, easygoing gent. Not a bit of your extroverted, loud-mouthed, aggressive reporter stereotype.

How does he *do* it, Jim??? *The Kandy-Kolored Tangerine-Flake Streamline Baby* (1965)? *The Pump House Gang* (1968)? *The Electric Kool-Aid Acid Test* (1968)? *Radical Chic & Mau-Mauing the Flak Catchers* (1970)? And his newest—out-mailering Mailer on NASA and the astronauts—to be called *The Right Stuff* (1974)? Here's how, Jim.

It is later that night at St. Lawrence. Everyone is just standing around the ol' Fireside Lounge in the UC—drinking coffee, eating cookies, waiting to see Tom Wolfe IN THE FLESH. Then we stroll in, Jim. Tom has on his deep-sea navy-blue suit now with lapels to the shoulders and four-button sleeves. He has his white linen shirt with a matched knit tie and the matched blue side-striped socks, and, to top it all off, Jim, the campiest of gold crescent Man-in-the-Moon tie studs as big as a Florida cockroach. Tom and I stand there in the middle of the room, and the students start to sidle over and crowd around.

Then it starts, Jim. Tom is just sort of standing there in the middle of the crowd, see, relaxed—why, he might as well have been humming the Budweiser beer song to himself—Hum hum humm hummm hummmm. . . . And everybody is suddenly telling him their life stories: childhood experiences, acid trips, boring, funny, incoherent—a whole crowd suffering from information compulsion, just pouring it all out; and Tom is just standing there, quietly smiling, listening, listening, nodding, taking it all in—clickity-click-click-click-click—with that mind of his. That's it, Jim. That's the magic.

Later yet, we get to talking about the novel again. I wonder, Jim. In spite of all this stuff about the new journalism, does Tom really secretly burn to write a novel himself? It's *true*, he *is* writing a novel. Tooooooooo freaking much! And, Jim, you know what he's calling it? *Vanity Fair!!!!!!*

JOE DAVID BELLAMY: Your position of advocating a revival of more or less Balzacian sensibilities and social concerns for fiction writers seems diametrically opposed to most of the credible theoreticians and practitioners. John Barth, for instance, predicts that "irrealism" rather than any sort of documentary realism is apt to be one of the more fertile areas of exploration.

TOM WOLFE: Well, I think Barth is a very good example of someone who is so excessively conscious of the history of the novel. In fact, I read a piece by him not too long ago in an anthology called *The Novel since World War II* in which he's painfully conscious of the idea of "avant-gardism" and of keeping it out on a frontier. I'm all for that, but I think the idea of a frontier today has become restricted to a sheerly formal frontier. In other words, it's true in every branch of the arts that the only frontier artists *believe* exists is the frontier of manipulating form. That's why painting, for example, has gone through such convulsions until now. Of course, it's no longer painting but "concept art" and "earth art," etc. Each of these has a life of about eighteen months—this frantic, hassling, speeded-up search for the new form. I think people are unconsciously selling themselves short when they want to make the form do the work....

The fact that there might be something new in content, or new in *comment*, is not anything that impresses people once they get into this frame of mind that the avant-grade is on the frontier sheerly of form.

BELLAMY: It's interesting that most of these same writers *would* agree with you that the novel is dead. But the novel they're talking about is the realistic novel. Whereas I suspect that when you say that the novel is dead, you would be saying that the fiction they're trying to write, which embodies a kind of diverse onslaught *against* the realistic novel, is what's dead.

WOLFE: It *is* dead, and it is very unfortunate that they should be spending so much energy on it. Because they've tricked themselves. They've gone through the history of aesthetics, and so forth, and they've said, "Because Proust did this much, and Henry James did this much, and James Joyce did this much, I can't do *those* things. They're not available to me. So what is there left?" So you really have to assume a very esoteric frame of mind in order to find out what's left.

That's one reason that the fact that journalism has no traditions is important to me. There are really no traditions in journalism worth observing. It's a low-rent form—always has been a low-rent form—and there's always been room for a lot of brawling about and a lot of mistakes. That's why, in a way, I shouldn't even go around giving talks about the new journalism; because if enough good writing comes out of the genre, people are eventually going to start becoming very self-conscious, just as novelists are now. They're going to be like Barth, who really does think acutely about what has already been done with the form of the novel. But if you think that way, obviously you're going to paint yourself into a corner. I would imagine that John Hawkes is in the same frame of mind, and a lot of younger writers certainly are in that frame of mind. I mean, I don't know Brautigan, but I'm sure he's probably thinking that way—just this tremendous fascination with Hermann Hesse, for example.

BELLAMY: Of course, the way you are going, the skills you're practicing and the forms that you're using aren't really disassociated from all of this. You call journalism a low-rent form, but you're obviously a very high-rent writer at this point and figure *into* this in my estimation of things. It occurs to me, for example, that your formulation about Balzac, even mentioning Balzac—I mean aside from his coffee and his writing habits—but actually mentioning Balzac as a figure to reflect upon seriously, is either, it seems, extremely prosaic or extremely avant-garde.

WOLFE: Well, I call this second-convolution avant-gardism. I think the novel is. . . . The novel is not dead. It's only the novelists who are strangling themselves on what is now a very orthodox, conventional aesthetics based on form. And there are no novelists today who are considered "talented" who would want to do what Balzac did, or what Thackeray or Dickens did. Their reason being: *they* did it. Why should we do it again? But the fact is that Balzac, Dickens, and Thackeray were not living in such an incredible period! Every period, I suppose, is incredible if you really get to the heart of it. But certainly *this* period—still—has so many undiscovered corners. There's so much *terra incognita* that novelists should be getting into that they could easily be wholly concerned with the social fabric, the social tableau. Forget the ersatz psychology that they get into.

BELLAMY: Of course, that's what you *are* getting into, sketching out of subcultures. . . .

WOLFE: Well, I've done what I can so far, and, well, I've done what I've done. I've completely relished this *terra incognita*, these subcultures, these areas of life that nobody wanted to write about— because they thought either they didn't know about them or they were beneath serious consideration. I imagine the most serious subject now is changes in the way people live, not politics, not wars. I think it's just the changes in the way people live, the changes in the way they look at the world. Perhaps that's always been the most serious subject.

BELLAMY: It comes down to the form-content distinction again, doesn't it? You're arguing that the content is always changing, so the same form is viable forever. Because the times are always changing, the content is always important. It's not just the form that is so crucially important.

WOLFE: I think this is absolutely true. You do have two new elements always available. You've got your own priceless, unique way of looking at things. Emerson said everybody has a great autobiography if he can only separate what is uniquely his experience from everybody else's. You've got *that* that's new anyway because you're born with it. It's just a question of whether you can put it down on paper. You're not looking at the world the same way as any other person, unless you've let yourself be so totally conditioned that you're some kind of automaton. But also—the second element—the conditions *around* you have changed. I think it's only the artist who is willing to face up to both forms of newness who is going to do major work, particularly at this point in history when the novelists have all crowded into one phone booth. They're just all in there. It's like some kind of a stunt. It's a shame.

Actually I say it's a shame, but I don't care because it makes things much easier for me. Really, I've had just a wide-open field; and it's just been marvelous. There's been no competition. All the people who would have been writing about the changes in "the way we live now"—that's Trollope's term originally—have just been off doing these poor, frantic, little exercises in form. I really have had so little competition—not just me, but other journalists who have concerned themselves with the way we live now.

You see, the irony is that despite all the aesthetic arguments, in the course of time the novelists—we'll just talk about novelists and forget the journalists—the *novelists* who are great, who are considered the great figures from their particular era, tend to be people who are performing this sort of news-bearing function. In 1970, which was the hundredth anniversary of Dickens' death, I believe, a great round of books, reviews, articles went on in England during which it was pretty conclusively decided that Dickens was *the* great figure in the English novel. The number two figure after Shakespeare. That's really sort of how this particular competition came out. Now this is a hundred years later, so this may be the final standings—since they start listing them in October after the baseball season is over. Dickens was hardly even reviewed by the serious journals in his own time. He was constantly downgraded as a topical writer. The same thing was true of Balzac. Balzac, for example, was never inducted into the French academy. Also, he generally got bad reviews. In Russia, well, Tolstoy probably outranks Dostoyevsky. There may be a little controversy there. And Tolstoy, again, was the news-bearing novelist. Gogol ranks very high, also a man giving the social tableau of his times. Gogol, Dostoyevsky, and Tolstoy finish in the money in that country.

BELLAMY: And Chekhov ... who also ... brought the news.

WOLFE: You're right. Chekhov . . . of course, he did, too.

BELLAMY: Of course, the argument that certain critics would make, you know, in conjunction with the death of realism, or at least of the nineteenth-century novel, is that the form of the community as it existed in the nineteenth century doesn't exist anymore —the dissolution of the organic commuity. So we have a fragmented society on our hands. There is no way you *could* get it in some kind of comprehensive picture. You have to go around doing subcultures, and isn't that a fragmented thing to do or something . . . ? You can't do all of America.

WOLFE: This is an argument that Trilling presented, and it's also an argument that a lot of novelists believe. Mailer believes this. He wrote a piece called "Some Children of the Goddess" in which he said that the novelist had to make a choice today whether he was going to follow the route of Dostoyevsky or Tolstoy, the idea being that Tolstoy presented the tableau of society in his time and Dostoyevsky turned you inward and toward the psychological dimension. I don't think it can be broken down that way, because Dostoyevsky, for example, dealt with an awful lot of social fabric of his time. But nevertheless, novelists believe this now, and they think you have to choose—and that since you don't have a coherent class structure, you can't write a novel that's going to be illustrative or symbolic of something larger, because it's all so fragmented. You write about this fragment, and all you can capture is just this fragment rather than the whole society.

I think all this is just an elaborate way of saying that the novelists don't understand the society, so they've abdicated looking at it. They've abdicated from the task of looking at it, I should say. And this impels a turn towards fantasy, the psychological novel, the "my first wife" novel. They've all turned towards Dostoyevsky—or Joyce, particularly. We're all, in one way or another, sons of James Joyce. This has just left us all a whole other area for nonfiction writers to make sense out of. But the idea of saying you can't make sense out of it or you can't present it in a way that gives people a larger picture of themselves is just inventing an excuse for avoiding a very difficult task. Sure, it's more difficult now. When you don't have a coherent class structure, it's more difficult to present a picture of the society. It's also more of a challenge, I think. That's why I think: here is a great frontier. It awaits, you know, somebody. All these novelists always talk about changing the consciousness of their times, but they're not even going to come close to it in the kinds of novels they're writing now. You know, there is no novelist in this country, no one who is still writing, who has had an original thought, an original insight into the society, because they insist on being romantic novelists who have a romantic view of their role. ...

BELLAMY: It occurs to me that for future historians if one wanted to get a picture of the twenties one might read Fitzgerald; if one wanted to get a picture of the sixties, let's say, one might read Wolfe. ...

WOLFE: [Spoken in jest with a British accent] I would certainly go along with that myself. . . .

BELLAMY: I mean, I wonder why it is that in the twenties you have the novel form predominating as a historical vehicle, whereas in the sixties you have the nonfiction form—what you might *call* the nonfiction form. Can you visualize what a form of the seventies might be, if it were still Wolfean? Would it be, *could* it be a novel? What kind of novel would it really be?

WOLFE: It could still be done *in* the novel. I think that the only future for the novel is reporting, which means there's not going to be *much* difference between the best novels and the best nonfiction. It's going to get down to a matter of technique. In fact, I'm having this battle with myself right now on this *Vanity Fair* book I told you about. I want to do a book that performs something of the same function of Thackeray's *Vanity Fair*, and I'm weighing whether this should be fiction or nonfiction, because everything in it is going to be based on a journalistic reality. Now, the question is to me a completely technical one. Once I reach that decision, the rest is purely technical.

The novel as a form no longer has any fascination for me as something that is a superior literary form. It's just a way of dealing with reality. And it has certain advantages. You can be more compact in a novel, in the sense that you can have one character express the roles or reality of two or three people in real life, because if they're similar people you can combine characteristics. You have much more liberty in dealing with the psychology of persons other than yourself. You know, you can do it in nonfiction; you have to interview people . . . you have to gain their confidence, interviewing at tremendous length before you can start getting them to tell you about their thoughts and to really level with you about their emotions. It can be done. It can be done much more economically in fiction.

Nonfiction has the advantage of the reader knowing that it's real. Now this is a tremendous thing—it sounds like nothing—but it's a tremendous thing to know that you're reading something that actually happened. That's why memoirs have always been so popular. You get all the advantages of a novel, and yet you know, or you assume, that it's true.

So, with this book I'm working on now it's a great technical problem. I call it a technical problem because it's sheerly, as far as I'm concerned, a matter of what is going to make the thing most real, what is going to give it the force, the richest presentation of the sort of life in our times. I'm not ashamed to be attempting to show the world "life in our times." We were talking about Balzac earlier: he was proud to be known as, and in fact referred to himself as, "the secretary of French society." It was the kind of term that no serious novelist today would be caught dead being stuck with.

I mean, anything but that. Because the novel now has the status that poetry had in the nineteenth century. It's the medium of the holy beast.

BELLAMY: Could you say some more about *Vanity Fair*?

WOLFE: Well, what Thackeray did was to try in one book to present the picture of ambition and status strife as he saw it in the London of his time. London, at that time, was really at its highest tide, because the British Empire was going strong and the money was pouring into England. He was presenting a picture of the great world capital of its time. And *nobody* has tried to do this for New York in our own time, despite the fact that New York has certainly been one of the most bizarre world capitals that has ever been. I mean, it's an extraordinary period we have lived through and are still living through—in everything from styles of behavior to fundamentals of behavior—the disruption and breakdown of whole class structures and everything else. I think novelists have been very afraid of New York as a subject. It's too big, too complicated. You really can't grasp it.

BELLAMY: Do you think that the subject of status, which is implied by the title *Vanity Fair* and has also been a recurring subject for you, is your main territory or interest?

WOLFE: I consider that as such a fundamental subject. It's really more of an analytical tool than a subject per se. It's just so fundamental to everything that people do that it's going to come up. That's the first thing I always look for.

The subject really irritates a lot of people. Some people basically think that to approach things with the idea of status in mind is in itself a rather snobbish way to look at things. People can also get very tired of the term very quickly, I've noticed.

BELLAMY: It tends to force them to face their own status, for one thing.

WOLFE: Well's it's just *the* fundamental taboo, more so than sexuality and everything of that sort. It's much easier for people to talk about their sex lives in this day and age than it is to talk about their status. I mean, just ask someone once to rank themselves socially, and you see someone squirm. It would certainly make me squirm. I wouldn't want to sit there and do it. I wouldn't want to do it in an honest way. I think my reaction would be to make a joke and avoid doing it.

BELLAMY: Getting back to the discussion of realism vs. fantasy, isn't the real crux of the issue the question of the nature of reality itself? It seems to me that one argument that's been given in favor of the new journalism is that so-called outside reality doesn't really exist, that all you really have is subjective reality. So the reporter, instead of using the old rigid forms and formulas, which were supposedly a way of capturing outside reality, assumes now that he's being more honest by giving his subjective experience, which he sees as truer to reality. And isn't that really the argument that the new novelists are giving too—that there is no "outside reality"? So that leaves you open to go into fantasy—because that's part of what really is, after all, because fantasy is part of reality. We're *always* having fantasies.

WOLFE: I disagree with that totally. Because, for my money, the only thing new in this new journalism I'm talking about is the new techniques that nonfiction writers have discovered they can use. The subjectivity that I value in the good examples of the new journalism is the use of techniques to enable the writer to get inside the subjective reality—*not* his own, but of the characters he's writing about. In other words, to use stream of consciousness so that I can present the mind of Ken Kesey—as I try to do in a number of chapters of *The Electric Kool-Aid Acid Test*—to get completely inside Kesey's mind, based on interviews, tapes that he made, or letters that he wrote, diaries, and so on. It's still a controversial thing to use, but I was not at all interested in presenting *my* subjective state when confronted with the Pranksters or whatever they had done. It was rather to try to get Kesey's completely. Same way in *Radical Chic & Mau-Mauing the Flak Catchers*. I do occasionally go inside the minds of other people, as I did with the inside of Leonard Bernstein's mind briefly, here and there.

This is quite different from saying that reality is so elusive that

whatever *I* feel is reality. Because—you're not just writing for yourself. I think this attitude becomes a form of taking the easy way
out. Honestly, there is *not* just one reality. But there are certain
things that are objectively known. For example, I am convinced
that everyone sees the color red the same way. There is no proof
of this, but I am convinced that it's true. I'm convinced that people
sense thickness, lightness, and so on, all in the same way. There *is*
this, I think. The externals are the same for everyone. Obviously,
people receive this "intracranially," as the brain physiologists say,
in different ways. But you can't dismiss the common denominators
in the external world and say that there is no reality. Because that's
just not true.

BELLAMY: I think that some of the writers I've talked to might
argue with you that your concept of objective reality is actually
the concept of reality that we've gotten from a certain art form,
which was the form of the nineteenth-century novel. That is, they
might argue, you are seeing reality in terms of the nineteenth-
century novel, whereas reality can actually be seen in all sorts of
different forms. Of course, you're right that these people are trying
to do what Joyce was trying to do in many ways, seeing reality in
a different way, as, let's say, made up of fantasy, made up of dis-
continuity, and that sort of thing. That may not be just "subjective
experience," but it actually may be what so-called outside reality
consists of.

WOLFE: Well, I mean, I think that concept of theirs is total
nonsense. It's egotism, really. It's very flattering to yourself to think
that your interior concept of reality is the only one that has any
meaning. In a way, Freudianism has conditioned us to think that.
Because Freud's great insight was that a person's own concept of
reality can be more crucial in his decisions than objective circumstance. As a matter of fact, Freud successfully forestalled advances
in brain physiology for fifty years—because people believed that
subjective states were that big a part of life. I don't think there's
any question but that eventually, scientifically, through research

into the central nervous system, they'll find out the actual facts of
the matter, or the best there is. Bishop Berkeley was wrong. If you
kick a tree, then your foot hurts. Eventually no one will have to
argue the fact that there *was* a tree there and your foot did hurt.
I think only aesthetes argue about it now. There is a very prosaic,
common, external reality, which is filtered through something
called your brain. Then you express, you make, your reaction in
various ways. Now obviously, as far as we know, there are no two
identical brains. There are no two absolutely identical conscious-
nesses. But this is not to say that the only reality is the internal
situation of the individual. I think all great writing somehow
knows this. All great writers know this in some way, and they take
the external world for what it is. And they also recognize the
complexity of internal states.

One Flew Over the Cuckoo's Nest is a good example. I don't
know what Kesey's thoughts are on this particular subject, but he
tells a tale through the eyes of a schizophrenic Indian. Sometimes
the Indian is lucid; sometimes he's crazy. Kesey changes these back
and forth to very good advantage, really to illustrate the very point
I'm talking about. Sometimes the Indian sees the elements of the
outside world very clearly, that is, the world outside of his skull,
that affect him in a very rational way: the fact that he is in prison,
the fact that he's treated like a secondary form of humanity, and
so on. Other times he's completely inside of his cranium. He's
imagining that fog has rolled into the hospital unit; he imagines
that the pills, the tranquilizers, have a machine inside of them that
controls his conduct. He switches off between the external reality
and the internal reality, but in a very conscious way—not the way so
many novelists do it, which is to hike themselves into the belief that
there is only one reality which is that inside of their skulls.

Now to just turn it around, let's look at it through the eyes of
the reader for a minute. A reader will put up with a lot, and a reader
will try to make sense out of any internal state that the writer has.
But eventually he's going to want the guy to "for God's sake, meet

me halfway," because we all know that there is a common meeting ground known as external reality. Show me enough of it so I know what terrain we're on.

That's why, in the case of Barthelme, a case of a writer whose work I admire, it's very hard for him to write at length. As long as he's writing in a short space, I think people can enjoy the intracranial exercise he's putting you through. I think *he* has tried to face up to that. I think the longest thing he's written has been *Snow White*, which was not his most successful work but perhaps his least successful. He's much better in a shorter space.

In a way, this is like the argument about form and content in painting. In painting, there's been a great animus against the literary. In fact, for years people were downgrading the literary elements, which merely meant the pictorial elements. Even when pop art came in, it was not considered pictorial painting. It was considered to be the denaturing of the banal units of the environment! There was a lot of sheer bullshit invented in order to justify pop art. To me, it seems very obvious that in painting you could have in one form, in one canvas, one painting, something that expressed both exciting form, such as shapes, color, use of space—to use one of the real bullshit words of modern aesthetics—*and* literary content. As in the case of Rembrandt. Since Rembrandt existed in the past, he can be ruled out, or El Greco, or Toulouse-Lautrec.

BELLAMY: Just because an idea is an old idea doesn't mean it's a bad idea.

WOLFE: Well, you see, *there* you have painters who are combining what is an external reality, which is things that exist, things you can see, things you can sense, *with* their own imaginations. And now, I think, the aesthetic has reached the point where people have been saying for so long: "It's only the intracranial activity that's important." Well, it may be the only thing that's important to the artist, but it's not the only thing important to the audience. The audience desperately wants to be able to make a pattern out of what it really is they're looking at.

That's why, as much as I admire a lot of the things that Burroughs has done, I use his work like a book of wallpaper samples. I like to dip into it to see techniques, and I've stolen a few here and there. I don't enjoy particularly reading anything straight through, because I feel that he's working behind a veil. He's put some kind of a veil up in front of what actually happened to him. Then he gives me a shadow show behind the veil, and he asks me to fill in the missing links and spaces. This can be very exciting up to a point. But if you reach that point after a few pages, after that you want him to level with you and say, you know, "what happened?" You can tell that he is describing what, I imagine, were things that happened to him, but he doesn't want to come out and really tell you. He makes it very cryptic, and he sort of parades symbols in front of you. He makes, in the long run, a rather artistic exercise out of it.

A different approach, although Burroughs probably thinks he's very close to these people, would be Henry Miller in *Tropic of Cancer*, a book I admire very much, or books such as *Journey to the End of Night* or *Death on the Installment Plan*, which is my favorite book title. These guys may be lying through their teeth, but you have the feeling that you're being leveled with—and that the writer is not denying you his picture of the external reality in order just to play these intracranial games. You have a feeling that he's really trying to show you the external reality *plus* the way the show ran inside of his cranium.

BELLAMY: Well, what is it then that you *get* with this leveling? That is, isn't it really Celine's perception of the world, which is different from somebody else's, or Miller's perception of the world? And isn't that, in a sense, really the result of his ability to imagine the world better than somebody else does?

WOLFE: Oh, sure, that's a crucial thing. But if he is also not showing you something new in the external world, or giving you a new insight. . . . Let's put it this way: he should also be giving you the thrill of recognition, as Dickens constantly did. I mean, people have been in court. They've been frustrated by their experiences in court. But when they read Dickens, they recognized the scene and then they said, "Oh, so *that's* the way it worked. *That's* why I felt frustrated!" It wasn't a new scene to them, but they got the thrill of recognition and an explanation of what was happening to them. Or, they got a look at a new world completely—the world of the English public school, or a better example would be the world of thieves that he presented in *Oliver Twist*.

BELLAMY: How about Zola as a model? Is that the kind of model of the new documentary writer who you say we need? Zola went out and took minute notes about the details of coal mines when he was writing *Germinal*.

WOLFE: Well, there you would have, yeah—the fact that he was bringing you news was a very important thing.

BELLAMY: Do you think that's enough? Isn't that Arthur Hailey really?

WOLFE: That's right, it is. The best thing is to have *both*—to have both someone who will bring you bigger and more exciting chunks of the outside world *plus* a unique sensibility, or rather a unique way of looking at the world, a unique fantasy life, even, to use the way Freud explains it, a unique emotional reality of his own that somehow echoes or vibrates with the emotional states of the reader. So that you get both the external reality and the subjective reality.

I'm not denying the existence of a subjective reality. Far from it. I'm just saying that there is also an objective reality that everyone in the world has to deal with. So I think you want to get the fullest experience that you can. That's why I think that the great painting of the future, as of the past, is going to be pictorial—illustration. Illustration done with an exciting use of form, as Rembrandt did it, as Toulouse-Lautrec did it, for that matter, as Dali has done it. ...

BELLAMY: So you don't believe the argument that the camera has made representational painting obsolete, or that, say, movies have made certain kinds of novelistic reality obsolete, the documentary kind of reality that you might get in some novels?

WOLFE: No, I think again this is just an argument that the novelists will tend to use to avoid both hard work and embarrassing work. Reporting is hard, and it's embarrassing.

BELLAMY: It's not for introverts?

WOLFE: Well, there are plenty of introverts who force themselves to do it. I mean, it can be done. It's hard, it's time-consuming, but the main resistance is: it doesn't seem artistic. Until people get over the idea that artistic excellence is separate from content, the novel is going to get painted into a smaller and smaller corner.

BELLAMY: How about Stephen Crane as an ideal of the way the novelist should behave? You know, a writer who had the sensibility and the equipment, but who also went out after material very much in the way of a reporter. His trip west, for example, on the train. He decides he wants to do western stories, so he hops on a train, takes a ride out west, and does "The Bride Comes to Yellow Sky" and things like that. Would that be your ideal of what a novelist, let's say, might do now if he wished to fill in this conspicuous gap in contemporary fiction?

WOLFE: That would certainly be the modus operandi, as they say in the police department. Mark Twain tended to do that.

BELLAMY: What do you make of the whole rash of autobiographies that are being written, books which once might have been called first novels except that the people who write them now decide to leave their names in? Or books like *Up* by Ronald Sukenick, for example, which is very much *like* that? I mean, it's very autobiographical, although some of it isn't. Sukenick calls the main character "Ronald Sukenick" and so on, but there's so much fantasy in there, so much stretching of the "truth" that he ends up calling it a novel anyway.

WOLFE: Well, in a way, that's what Henry Miller did. That's what Celine did. Celine would lead you to believe that everything in his novels happened to him. In fact, a lot of it did, but he also gives himself the license to depart from the facts when he wants to.

There's a great confusion now. The novelists are so conscious of literary history, always so self-conscious that they're all reading

their literary histories trying it find out what's left. And I guess
it's just an age of nonfiction. So you have events like Herbert Gold
writing a novel called *Fathers* in which the two fathers in the book
are Herbert Gold, Sr. and Jr., and from all the external facts of his
life I presume it's his father and himself. He calls this a novel, and
I presume this just means that when he got to certain situations if
he wanted to change the facts he did so. In Gore Vidal's recent
book *Two Sisters* there are two characters in there: one is Gore
Vidal, called Gore Vidal; one is his sister, called by her name; and
there are some fictional characters, one of whom is apparently
based on Jacqueline Kennedy; then there's a straight essay in the
middle. Capote's new book, *Answered Prayers*—I don't know exactly what it's going to be, but if in fact it is using real people with
their real names in fictional situations, again you have this kind of
curious blending. William Styron, writing *The Confessions of Nat
Turner*, is an example of this. I think, ten years ago, somebody
might have written *The Confessions of Nat Blender* based on the
life of Nat Turner.

This is happening because the novel is so confused and novelists
very uncertain of what's going on. They still want to be known as
novelists. When Capote wrote *In Cold Blood*, for instance, he made
sure that everyone knew he considered it a novel. He called it a
nonfiction novel. It was very important to him that it would not be
called journalism, but a novel, a nonfiction novel. It made me
laugh because this is exactly what Fielding had gone through at
the very beginnings of the novel in English. It was very important
to him that *Joseph Andrews* and *Tom Jones* be called "comic epics
in prose." The epic had been the great form prior to Fielding's
time, so he was saying, in effect, "I'm not writing one of these
novels; I'm writing a comic epic in prose." So people did get hung
up on the prestige of a certain form before the novelists. All of
them would have been much better off if they had never read a
literary history.

BELLAMY: What sort of impact do you see the electric media

making—if I can ask a McLuhanesque question—on writing forms?
Do you think there is a valuable cross-fertilization going on?

WOLFE: No. I used to wonder about this a great deal. There's no
question that electric media have had an effect, mostly an effective
usurpation. Obviously television and the movies, film of various
sorts—when you talk about television you're talking about film, by
and large—has usurped a lot of the functions of short stories, novels.
One thing, however, that no electric medium can do so far—somebody may find a way to do it—is the interior monologue, or just
simply "point of view." You don't have to give it such a name. But
the real point of view, in which the audience feels that it is inside the
mind, or the central nervous system, of a character—movies have
never been able to do this. They can do everything else, and they
can do it better. They can establish a locale much more economically and in a much more striking way, in a way you'll never forget.
They *cannot* get inside of characters. They've tried every sort of
thing. They've tried voice-overs, they've tried shooting from behind
the head of a character, they've tried making the camera like a pair
of eyes in which the main character only sees himself in a mirror.
That was done in one movie. I forget the name of it.

The closest thing was in the movie *Alfie*, which used the aside.
It came closer than anything else. Michael Caine, who was Alfie,
would occasionally turn toward the camera and deliver a comment
on what he was doing. For some weird reason that I can't figure
out psychologically, this worked much better than anything else.
You really have much more of a feeling of being inside a character.
On stage this is simply an aside. It doesn't work terrifically on the
stage either, because obviously the guy's not aside. There are a lot of
people around him. But anyway, even that didn't do what a novel
can do in terms of making you feel like you're inside somebody's
head. Or what nonfiction can do. I did it in a number of chapters
in *The Electric Kool-Aid Acid Test*. John Sack did it in his book
on Vietnam.

BELLAMY: I was going to say that, of course, *you're* doing that

all the time. You're always getting *inside* of characters, and you do
it without announcing it in any way. You just zip inside of somebody, even sometimes for just a second. I think of the line in "The
Put-Together Girl," you know, where you say, "Carmen is very
social." For that one line you're getting inside the mother's head.
You just drop that, you know, and that's it. You're inside of her
head, and then you zap right out again. You're always doing that,
like a whirling dervish. It seems to me that, in the form that you use,
you get inside and outside of characters quicker and more subtly
than most novelists do. That's probably the most characteristic piece
of virtuosity one finds in your work.

WOLFE: Well, actually, you're the first person I've run into who
seems to have realized what I was doing in that respect. Because it
is something I've done again and again. Even in expository sections
I often try to adopt the tone of a character. When I write about
Junior Johnson's stock car race, often I may be just describing a
race course or a carburetor or some damn thing, and I'll try to do
it in the language of Junior Johnson to create the feeling that you're
still within the person's point of view.

I really learned some valuable lessons in this from reading some
of the young Soviet writers—like the brothers Serapion. Most of
them are not well known. I guess the most famous would be
Eugene Zamyatin, Boris Pilniak, and there's a guy, very seldom
remembered, called Andrei Sobol. Alexis Remizov is another one.
At any rate, they're all novelists or short story writers. They were
writing about the revolution, but they took a panoramic view, so
they didn't stick with one character usually. They were always
doing very tricky things with point of view. I became very conscious
of that sort of technique when I was at Yale. At graduate school I
discovered these guys just by roaming through the stacks at the
Yale library, all in translation, of course. I found that you can do
this in nonfiction to a great advantage. Just carefully manipulate
point of view. Your example was quite a good one.

That piece I did on Phil Specter—in the very beginning—it was
the first time I ever actually went inside of somebody else's mind. It

is one thing to do an interior monologue in your own mind. It's something else to do one in someone else's mind. In fact, it's quite a chance to take because the person may scream bloody murder, and you really don't have any defense except that you feel you're doing it accurately. You really feel you know the person well enough and what their state was in this particular incident or you don't. So I did it with Specter in his own plane. He was having paranoid reactions to the plane starting to take off, so he makes the plane stop. He makes them stop the whole flight and he gets off with a big furor. Afterwards, one of the news magazines—as they occasionally do—got into one of these anti-new-journalism spasms and called up Specter and a number of other people that I had written about and wanted to know if this was *accurate*, you know. Specter hadn't told me about the whole thing, but he said, "Yeah, that's exactly the way I felt at that time." I had never asked him myself, you know, what he thought of that particular thing. They also called up Jane Holzer, from the "Girl of the Year" story I did in my first book, and even went by her apartment to see if I had gotten all the details of the apartment correctly.

BELLAMY: I was going to ask you a question about the setup you have in "O Rotten Gotham," where you get up on the balcony with Edward T. Hall, looking down on Grand Central Station. Now, when I read that, it seemed to me that that was suitable license; that is, if you really didn't do that with Edward T. Hall, I would grant you the right to do that. But I wanted to ask you: *did* you actually go with Edward T. Hall up on the balcony?

WOLFE: Oh, yes. Absolutely. Down into the subways with him. If I remember that day, we first went to Grand Central. We did all that, went down in the subways, walked around in the middle of Manhattan a little bit; then *New York* magazine had hired a car. We got in the car. There was a driver so we could both talk and look at things, and we went all through Harlem and all over the place.

BELLAMY: If it hadn't happened, would you consider that to be an acceptable license? I mean, it seems to me that piece is utterly defensible for being a beautiful example of a first-rate popularization of important scientific information. By presenting Hall as a figure, a flesh-and-blood person, you've made it more approachable for people who wouldn't ordinarily be able to dig the scientific business, you know. But *would* you consider presenting that particular scene as justifiable license if you hadn't done that *because* it works dramatically?

WOLFE: It would be justifiable, if Hall had done it and I hadn't, to present Hall based on his recollection—without saying this is what Hall remembered, but just have him there.

BELLAMY: You would not put yourself next to him?

WOLFE: I would not put myself next to him if I had not been there. No. I'm expecting the reader to allow me a certain leeway *if* it leads towards a better grasp of what actually took place. In other words, I expect the reader to allow me to present what Hall might have done in that particular position without having a preamble that says, "I wasn't with this man at this time; but based on his memory of what took place, this was it." I expect the reader to grant me the right to present that without that preamble. I don't expect him, however, to grant me the right to make up anything. I think it kind of kills the whole thing.

BELLAMY: That's fiction, I guess.

WOLFE: Because part of the impact is the fact that you're telling the reader *this happened*. This is not a short story. This is not a novel. This is not fiction.

John Hawkes

INTERVIEWED BY ROBERT SCHOLES

For some years I have been interested in the fiction of John Hawkes, reading it with pleasure and writing about it with admiration. To my mind Hawkes is one of the small handful of contemporary novelists whose work really matters. His oeuvre now includes *The Cannibal, The Beetle Leg, The Lime Twig, Second Skin, The Innocent Party* (plays), and *Lunar Landscapes.* In the past years, since I joined Hawkes on the staff of the English department at Brown University, I have come to know him personally and to respect his integrity as a teacher and his kindness as a human being. The publication of his controversial new novel *The Blood Oranges* seemed an appropriate occasion to arrange a formal interview with him in which we could talk for the record about that book and related matters.

The interview took place on a hot summer afternoon in 1971 at Hawkes's house on a shady street in Providence, Rhode Island. He and I sat on the floor, on either side of a cool fireplace, with a dictaphone and a few cans of cold beer on the hearth between us. As we talked and sipped, young Hawkeses wandered in and out, and sometimes the soft, tidewater accents of Hawkes's wife Sophie could be heard in the background, speaking on the telephone or talking to the children.

In working on the transcription of the tapes we made that day I was struck repeatedly by how much got lost when the words Hawkes had spoken were separated from his voice. It is a powerful voice, with a brassy timbre, which expresses beautifully the warmth and conviction of the man. His words are eloquent, but those who only read them will be missing the music of their original delivery.

ROBERT SCHOLES: Now, after being known as a novelist of violence and the terrible, you have certainly in your latest novel, *The Blood Oranges*, proved to be a singer of love. How do you account for the change?

JOHN HAWKES: I'm tempted to say middle age, experience, education, living. But I'm not at all sure the change is as severe as it appears.

SCHOLES: I was wondering if you'd admit that there was a change at all. You seem *almost* willing to admit it. Is that right?

HAWKES: I think that the lyricism and idealism that Cyril sings in *The Blood Oranges* is implicit in everything I've written.

SCHOLES: Certainly the last section of your previous novel, *Second Skin*, had a similar kind of lyricism. But I think many people in reading *Second Skin* would have felt that that lyricism was entirely imaginary; a sense one has of the beautiful floating island in that book is of something unreal, while our sense of the dark, bitter northern island is real. Is this just because people have the wrong sense of reality?

HAWKES: I suppose it's a question of which kind of fictionally created reality strikes people the most powerfully. *Second Skin* is about the imagination. There is no doubt in *my* mind that Skipper's floating island is totally real. The landscape of the imagination is real in that fiction, whether it's projected as the idyllic, wandering tropical island or the rock-rooted, cold, barren New England island. I think that to write fiction that portrays the nightmarish aspects of the unconscious is simply to say at the outset that the opposite view is equally true and equally valid. All of my fiction is, in a sense, lyrical, even the most terrifying of it. The nightmare simply leads one toward—or the nightmare could not exist without an awareness of—purity. But even in the most paradisal of the worlds I've created, the roses conceal deadly thorns.

SCHOLES: I'm tempted to bring this discussion to a very plain vulgar level for a moment. *The Blood Oranges* is a novel about two couples, and in one sense it might crassly be called a novel about wife-swapping, which is apparently much practiced among our higher bourgeoisie today. Are you setting up in *The Blood Oranges* to advocate the new sexual freedoms promoted by *Playboy*, or what?

HAWKES: *The Blood Oranges* is about sexuality. But it is also about the imagination. *Wife-swapping, husband-swapping* are indeed vulgar terms. And yet they're interesting terms; they set up their own vibrations. Cyril is probably right when he says that monogamy is the enemy of marriage. That's not to say that marriage isn't essential, meaningful, poetic, perhaps the deepest experience we can imagine. I'm for marriage. I began to write when Sophie and I got married. Our marriage is thoroughly conventional. However, if we're speaking of life in general, rather than our own lives, to base the definition of marriage on sexual monogamy is absurdly reductive. Cyril's modest defiance of matrimonial conventions is intended to lead us into realities of the imagination. He is trying to talk about paradox, or the existence of that which does not exist.

SCHOLES: I know you and I both as college teachers are in touch with young people a lot, or people in that interesting phase between young and something else. I'm wondering if the view of sexual morality in *The Blood Oranges* has something to do with what's going on among the young, whether it is in some sense a response to changes one sees in the life around us or whether it is simply a working out of your own evolution as a writer.

HAWKES: I think that the relationship between what's going on in *The Blood Oranges* and what's going on among younger people in actual life around us is coincidental. The parallels certainly exist. The most interesting students I know are likely to view the word *adultery* with a kind of casual surprise or total indifference. I think that's a good thing. I think the word *adultery* is as odious as the phrase *wife-swapping*. Perhaps for a moment we should get back to the wife-swapping. I myself think that any form of sexual experience is probably desirable, probably has built into it human poetic excitements, fulfillments, joys. I don't like the phrase *wife-swapping*. I don't like the concept of "swapping." I don't think that sexuality should in fact be a matter of horse trading, which is why the term, if not the act, strikes us as vulgar. At any rate Cyril uses the phrase *sexual extension* (and again *The Blood Oranges*, like the rest of my fiction, is not autobiographical), and I think that I too believe in the concept of sexual extension. However, in the novel these ideas are really aimed at attempting to test our language, ourselves, our illusionary existence. They are there to provide us with some amusement as well as to evoke desire, joy, serenity, and horror.

SCHOLES: It seems to me that at a couple of moments in *The Blood Oranges* one detects in Cyril's voice a somewhat condescending or disapproving attitude toward the mere sexuality of polymorphous perversity among the young. Is Cyril's way a higher way, do you think, than something merely fleshly?

HAWKES: Cyril does have his moments of middle-aged defensiveness, which was one way of making him a comic character. But such moments are mild and good-natured. Cyril is not beyond fleshly experience. To him *fleshly* is a powerful, suggestive, provocative word. *Fleshly*, to Cyril, is not a vulgarized cliché (like *wife-swapping*). Cyril is himself fleshly, he wishes to eat even the ground he walks on, he loves everything and everybody.

SCHOLES: Well, I think that while we are into discussing Cyril, we might discuss the other three characters in the book just a little bit. Certainly Cyril's opposite in the book, Hugh, is opposite in every way; as Cyril is in some sense a libertine, Hugh is in some sense a Puritan, even though he and Cyril are both engaged in what we were vulgarly calling wife-swapping a moment ago. Am I right in seeing Cyril and Hugh as polarizing sensuous and puritanical life?

HAWKES: Absolutely. Cyril is pure, Hugh is a Puritan; Cyril to me is not a libertine but simply a God-like man with infinite capacities for love. Cyril is a modest but literal lover. Hugh is an idealist. And Hugh's idealism is a totally destructive quality. Cyril is a practitioner of Hugh's idealism, is able to love with the strength and purity that is in fact Hugh's ideal. Hugh's ideal, however, keeps him from loving at all. And it is Hugh's remoteness from love that causes his death, which in turn destroys the relationship or the harmony between all four characters. I think that for me those characters are indeed polar opposites, versions of a single figure; they are both artists.

SCHOLES: I don't find quite the same kind of opposition between the two women in the book that I see in Cyril and Hugh. I certainly do see the men the way you present them now. But the women, Fiona and Catherine, are opposite in some way, but I suspect in a much more subtle way. I must say I found them both very attractive, among the most attractive females in your fiction. So many of the others, at least the ones before Catalina Kate, had been terrible in the ultimate sense of that word. Do you yourself have a preference between Catherine and Fiona as an example of womanhood?

HAWKES: I think I ought to say, Bob, before we go any further, and again perhaps evading the question, that when Sophie, our daughter, read *The Blood Oranges* she said, "Oh, Dad, you are both Hugh and Cyril, aren't you?" And I said, "Ah, Sophie, I'm so happy you think so, but I'm afraid that actually I'm neither one." To get back to Catherine and Fiona, if you found those two characters equally engaging, then obviously the fiction achieved a certain success and I'm delighted. I think the task for me was to create a narrator who was able to perceive in any woman, whose life touched his own, the kind of beauty that would enable him to give back a corresponding beauty. It wasn't easy. Obviously certain writers have deliberately created unattractive women and have been able to portray their essential selves, their womanhood, their existence as females, in such a way as to engage the reader enormously and to make him perfectly aware of the characters' beauty. But I found it hard to make Catherine spiritually and physically beautiful when at the same time I was trying to portray her as merely housewife, merely burdened mother. The point is that she fulfills a conventional role, but at the same time responds to Cyril without a moment's hesitation, and it's the immediacy of her life that Cyril loves.

SCHOLES: Yes, I think in a way Catherine shares with Cyril a sort of powerful placidity which Hugh and Fiona lack. Fiona, being the obviously attractive, eternally girlish, beautiful Aphrodite in the novel, is somehow less solid than Catherine. And motherliness has its own sexuality, I suppose, which I think is conveyed very well in the book. It seems to me also that you do something interesting by suggesting at the end a motherliness in Fiona, or at any rate a willingness to assume that role with respect to Catherine's not too attractive children. Am I reading the novel right in that respect? Is there motherliness latent in Fiona all along?

HAWKES: Sure. I began to write this fiction out of the darkest, dark night, thinking that I might not be able to write again. Then suddenly I visualized a fragmented scene of some children carrying a coffin which contained a dead dog, and being followed by four adults, which was the beginning of *The Blood Oranges*. At that moment I was quite aware of *Twelfth Night*, that beautiful whole in which all of our fragmented selves are finally realigned into the ultimate harmony. In *The Blood Oranges* I wanted to strive toward precisely that kind of structure, so that the characters are all supposed to be versions of a single figure. And you're quite right that Catherine is the mother-version of Fiona; Fiona is the Aphrodite of Catherine. The two are probably one. Cyril is probably just as self-destructive as Hugh. Hugh in his death is at least probably as much the visionary as Cyril is. I was trying to deal with the components, the parts, the inadequate fragments of human nature.

SCHOLES: Could you say a little more about the genesis of the book?

HAWKES: As I said, *The Blood Oranges* began with a small vision, literally seen, but at the same time I was thinking of a couple of books and a couple of ideas that I've been concerned with for a long while. First there is the epigraph from *The Good Soldier* in the front of *The Blood Oranges*. And for a long time I had been thinking about a student who once questioned the validity of the moral vision of *The Lime Twig*. That is, in *The Lime Twig*, what Cyril would call sexual extension is punished by death and total cataclysmic collapse, which is the mighty backlash of my own Puritan upbringing. When the student, who happened to have been a marvelous girl, said, "Why can't Michael Banks in *The Lime Twig* simply have sex with all those women and go on living in an ordinary way?" I really had no answer. Similarly, I've heard students resist *The Good Soldier* because of the convention of adultery which is essential to that book. Once again, this is a fiction that I admire enormously but which portrays an enormously bleak future for any love that seeps out of the rigidities prescribed by marriage. When I began *The Blood Oranges* I was quite aware of trying to write a fiction that would offer a somewhat different version of Ford Madox Ford's novel and that would give me an alternative to *The Lime Twig*.

SCHOLES: In comparison with the work of other writers who are writing now and whom I admire, it seems to me that you are the most visual. Does this have something to do with your interest in dream and image?

HAWKES: My fiction is almost totally visual, and the language depends almost totally on image. I think you're quite right that this fictional preoccupation and this particular interest in language do depend on my feeling for dreams and on my interest in exploiting the richness and energy of the unconscious.

SCHOLES: You are one of the few contemporary writers mentioned favorably in a dreadful new work of criticism called *The Future of the Novel* by Anaïs Nin. I don't know whether you've seen that

or not, but she sees you as, in some way, carrying on the great tradition of the surrealists, and if you weren't a little violent—which she
deplores—you would probably have her wholehearted approval.
Do you think of yourself as related to André Breton and the surrealist tradition, or is this simply a coincidence?

HAWKES: I don't know much about the surrealists. I like and
respect Anaïs Nin and once introduced her at a *Harvard Advocate*
reading. I've read one book of André Breton's, *Nadja,* which I admired very much indeed, though it's not my kind of fiction because
it is literally dreamlike, murky, fluid—one moment of life slipping
syrupy, mucouslike into another. This is not my way. And that I am
not a surrealist writer ought to be pretty clear. However, I suppose
that I have an affinity with surrealism simply because of the felt
power of the dreamlike conflicts out of which I try to make narrative fiction.

SCHOLES: The question of dream is really a fascinating one. Perhaps we can get into it a little deeper while we're on it. As a matter
of writing practice, do you, in fact, try to use your subconscious, to
use dreams or reveries or other not strictly conscious things in your
actual working and writing?

HAWKES: Certainly not, Bob. As you well know, I believe in
coldness, detachment, ruthlessness, a lot of consciousness in the
choice of narrative material, in the creation of scenes and so on. It's
simply that in the process of writing my hope is to liberate the kind
of energy and to uncover the kinds of material that seem desperately and beautifully essential to us as readers.

SCHOLES: I wonder if we can talk a little bit about some of the
other images in *The Blood Oranges*, beginning with the image in
the title. Why the blood oranges?

HAWKES: To begin with, we spent a few months in France several years ago. That was the first time I'd been in Europe since the
Second World War. One of the marvelous French moments was
eating cheese; another was, for the first time, eating blood oranges.
The phrase came to mind as a title. The fruit is sweet, but it's

streaked with the color of blood, which to me is a paradox. It means that the blood is real but also sweet; it means that no sweetness is ephemeral but on the contrary possesses all the life-drive seriousness of the rich, black flow of blood itself. It suggests wound invading desire, desire "containing" agony.

SCHOLES: It certainly is a gorgeously succulent and sexual image for a title. I congratulate you on finding it. But your insistence on the paradox of sweetness and blood reminds me that the capacity to enjoy ugliness and to take a benign interest in the horrible is something that you set a very high value on, perhaps a higher value than anyone else I know or even know *of*. Do you sense that in doing this you are doing something rather special, rather different from what most people do?

HAWKES: Yes, I write for precisely those two purposes. But on the other hand, I should think that most serious writers have similar purposes. After all, trying to reveal the essential beauty of the ugly, trying to elicit our own potential for weakness, failure, is not so unusual. All interesting fiction attempts to extend our sympathies, to allow us to fulfill all of the characteristics which conventional society would repress and destroy. From Conrad to Shakespeare, obviously, these same impulses and motivations are true.

SCHOLES: In a way we've got to a point where larger questions seem to open up whether one wants to face them or not. I think back to the point at which we started, the question of the assault on traditional sexual morality which one could say the novel *The Blood Oranges* is, and I think of the questions of the public morality that keep coming up all the time and the relationship of fiction to these things. I'm never sure myself of the proper relationship between the imaginary world of the novel and the world of day-to-day living. I never know to what extent in a work of fiction I'm getting advice that may be put to use in my own life or getting some kind of alternative to my own life which is in some beautiful and deep way totally irrelevant. I wonder if you have any special feelings about the relationship of your own work to the lives of your readers. Are you offering a way out of the world or a way into the world?

HAWKES: I wouldn't think of it as offering ways in or out of the world. I write what I would like to read. I think that we read for joy, for pleasure, for excitement, for challenge. It would seem pretty obvious, however, that fiction is its own province. Fiction is a made thing—a man-made thing. It has its own beauties, its own structures, its own delights. Its only good is to please us and to relate to our essential growth. I don't see how we could live without it. It may be that the art of living is no more than to exercise the act of imagination in a more irrevocable way. It may be that to read a fiction is only to explore life's possibilities in a special way. I think that fiction and living are entirely separate and that the one could not exist without the other.

SCHOLES: I wonder in a way, and I suppose in a very ordinary way, whether one in the world of the living could achieve the gorgeous grace of Cyril with respect to sexuality, or whether one should attempt, let's say, to achieve the ideal set forth in the novel. In other words, this seems to me an ideal which is so ideal in fact, and Illyria a place which is so gorgeous in its way, that it almost prevents one from thinking of emulating it at all.

HAWKES: Gorgeous? As a matter of fact, the world of Illyria as described in *The Blood Oranges* actually consists of an arid landscape with a few broken-down stone huts, some villagers, a few boats, a lot of sun, a lot of desolation, some lemons, and four people. And here you are, Bob, sitting in a blue, short-sleeved shirt, a pair of striped, short, ragged trousers, an enormous grey-black beard, some hair sticking out of the side of your head, a smile that is enormous, eyes that are gleaming, a Protean man angled and at perfect ease in a corner of this room. You look like Cyril, you talk like Cyril, you live on the sea, you love, you're alive. So what are you talking about? *You* exemplify the possibility of living fully, honestly, truly, benignly, joyously. This is all my character does.

SCHOLES: Wow! Perhaps the *possibilities* exist in the day-to-day world, but the *actuality* exists in the world of Illyria and I can't help thinking that that name is a warning not to try to translate the values and virtues of that world into this world.

HAWKES: I disagree. I think that when Fiona asks Cyril where they are and he answers, "Sure . . . in Illyria," he is simply trying to designate the power, beauty, fulfillment, the possibility that is evident in any actual scene we exist in.

SCHOLES: I think I understand what you mean, that if one has the creative power one can somehow or other bring Illyria into being around one, at least to a certain extent.

HAWKES: Illyria doesn't exist unless you bring it into being.

SCHOLES: I get the picture. This, in a way, suggests some other concerns which I think we should talk about a little bit. The world of Illyria is, of course, a very small world, a very personal world, a world of four people, two marriages and their interaction. I take it from the intensity, the smallness, of this world and similar aspects of the world of your other fiction that you believe the main concerns of living are the small and personal as opposed, for instance, to the large, the political, the socially active. Is that a fair assessment?

HAWKES: A long time ago, Albert Guérard wrote that *The Cannibal* was not a political book but was a truer picture of our lives at the time of World War II than history itself. Illyria, you say, is a matter of two marriages and four people. Then you raise the question of the "big things"—politics. Well, we could say that *The Agamemnon* is merely a domestic tragedy concerning four principal characters. In a way, the elements of *Twelfth Night* are just as apparently limited. To me Illyria is not so small a world. But, of course, I would never begin a fiction with "big themes" in mind, would never work with them consciously—and yet surely my fiction is resonant with implications.

SCHOLES: Jack, I know that in addition to being a writer you are a teacher of young writers, if there is such a thing, and I know that this question of politics and its relation to creative writing or the writing of fiction is a thing that worries a lot of young writers. They find it difficult to justify the indulgence in the personal satisfaction of writing at a time when the calls to the barricades seem to come more frequently and more urgently every month. What do you do to reassure the young people, to keep them writing and off the barricades, or do you encourage them to go?

HAWKES: I think the acts of courage and the acts of creativity evident in the writing of fiction are similar to the qualities evident in revolutionary acts. I think clear vision, detachment, personal strength, selflessness—these are needed to change the world literally and, no doubt, are also essential to the imaginative act. The paradox is that the literary act can't take place in the context of revolution or "real life" or world activity. I would be willing to give up writing (which I began to discover only as a young person and not at the barricade but in the midst of the primordial, fluid, slippery, messy stuff of the Second World War)—I would be willing to give up art if the actual barricade were before us. If it were literally a moment of attempting to participate in those human efforts of planning and action that had to do with political ultimacy and finality, I would want to be there.

SCHOLES: In your fiction are you working out of a consciously held theoretical position?

HAWKES: Recently I did formulate a kind of theory of fiction which can be expressed in few words. It seems to me that fiction should achieve revenge for all the indignities of our childhood; it should be an act of rebellion against all the constraints of the conventional pedestrian mentality around us. Surely it should destroy conventional morality. I suppose all this is to say that to me the act of writing is criminal. If the act of the revolutionary is one of supreme idealism, it's also criminal. Obviously I think that the so-called criminal act is essential to our survival.

SCHOLES: Recently I saw W. H. Auden quoted as saying that the world would be exactly the way it is if Shakespeare and Dante and somebody else had never lived, which suggests a sort of beautiful irrelevance to art or, at any rate, an existence apart from political, geographical, geopolitical realities. Do you accept Auden's view?

HAWKES: Was he joking?

SCHOLES: I think he was serious. I assume this is a later version of his "poetry makes nothing happen."

HAWKES: Then he's filled with despair. I'm sympathetic with despair. I don't agree with the idea. It seems obvious that the great acts of the imagination are intimately related to the great acts of life—that history and the inner psychic history must dance their creepy minuet together if we are to save ourselves from total oblivion. I think it's senseless to attempt to talk as Auden talked. The great acts of the imagination create inner climates in which psychic events occur, which in themselves are important, and also affect the outer literal events in time and space through what has occurred in the act of reading.

SCHOLES: I know that in another interview you were quoted as saying something like, "Optimism is bad; pessimism is good." I found this comforting myself. I wonder if you could elaborate a little bit on why pessimism is better than optimism?

HAWKES: Optimism is an expression of the imperceptive. Pessimism is simply that view of the pained person who has perceived his own potentials for horror—within himself and also around himself in the contortions of living. Optimism is of course a totally shallow view. It is informed by nothing. One does not wish to be optimistic or hopeful. A person wants to live with a life-drive, with a sense of life-validity, having some notion of the vastness of human potential.

SCHOLES: I share your enthusiasm for pessimism, and yet it seems to me that some of your most interesting and engaging characters are incurable optimists; Skipper certainly would have to go in that category. You would think that life would have made a pessimist of Skipper, but it didn't, and I would say that Cyril also is incredibly optimistic. Perhaps not incredibly but credibly optimistic.

HAWKES: Okay, Bob. We're not going to get back to this optimistic, pessimistic business. We can't deny the essential crippling that is everywhere in life. I don't advocate crippling; I'm an opponent of torture. I deplore the nightmare; I deplore terror. I hap-

pen to believe that it is only by traveling those dark tunnels, perhaps not literally but psychically, that one can learn in any sense
what it means to be compassionate. I don't hope for anything. To
want to live and write has nothing to do with hoping. Most of us
are trying to create things that never existed before. You don't do
this on hope.

SCHOLES: *The Blood Oranges* is the least terrible of your works,
I think, though obviously terror is still important to you and it's
present in that work as it is in the others. But I wonder about the
mellowness of *The Blood Oranges*, and I wonder about the aston-
ishing glow that is generated in that book. I keep thinking about the
whole course of your works—from *The Cannibal*, which is, I suppose, the most terrible. It does seem that you have moved the way
Dante moved, through hell, purgatory, and into something like
paradise in the Illyria of *The Blood Oranges*. Of course the obvious
question is where do you go from here?

HAWKES: Do you think I've finished?

SCHOLES: I wonder if you go back to hell or if there is a paradise
beyond paradise?

HAWKES: I've always been bored with Dante's *Paradiso*. An aca-
demician wrote me after *Second Skin* and said, "Where do you go
after this hymn of pure beauty?" I didn't know. I was grateful for
the implied compliment. I was filled with despair by the implied
ending. However, I love language, I believe in the illusion of total
sexuality, I defend the absolute truth of the brutality of the nightmare.

SCHOLES: Are you troubled at all by the idea of writing better
and better for fewer and fewer people?

HAWKES: I'm writing better and better but not for fewer and
fewer people. Let's get back to wife-swapping.

SCHOLES: The wife-swapping "angle" in *The Blood Oranges*
could be seen as an attempt at popularization. Are you trying to
compete with *The Love Machine*, *The Exhibitionist*, and similar
vulgarizations of sexuality?

HAWKES: I think that wife-swapping is at the thematic center of the novel. I hadn't thought of the subject as leading to popular appeal. That's not the point. Again, I think, on the other hand, Bob, that most people reading *The Blood Oranges* wouldn't really think of that fiction in terms of *wife-swapping*. The phrase itself suggests a kind of banality, a kind of mindlessness, casualness, which *The Blood Oranges* probably doesn't evoke. All the time we've been talking, I've had this sorry lingering sensation that I may have been condescending in my reaction to the phrase *wife-swapping*, which is, after all, a pretty common phrase. Certainly it's chauvinistic. It seems to me that it's a matter of definition. If, by "wife-swapping" or "husband-swapping" you meant some form of expression and behavior that was tender, considerate, humane, poetic, joyous, ecstatic, reasonable, and unhurtful, and if you were talking about a kind of activity that was not malicious and not revengeful—if all of that is implied in that (I still think) ugly phrase *wife-swapping*, then of course I couldn't be more sympathetic. And, as a matter of fact, as a person and writer I would have to be sympathetic. Even if "wife-swapping" meant the opposite, even if it did mean exploitation, or a kind of nightmare, desperate effort to keep alive, even if it meant mere casualness, meant the shabbiest kind of bad taste, poverty of spirit, poverty of flesh, of course, I would ultimately be sympathetic to the people involved. I would rather have "wife-swapping" than sterility. I would rather have "wife-swapping" than nothing. You and I may be spared such desperateness.

SCHOLES: Do you think then, that there is some hope for evolution in sexual relationships, that some kind of life-style which involves perhaps communal relationships, or at any rate something different from standard monogamous marriage, is a real possibility for the present and the future?

HAWKES: Maybe while our generation leads the world to disaster a vast horde of thirty-year-olds will be leading it toward a kind of colorful consummation.

SCHOLES: For our last question, let's get back to the concrete or the "metal" details of *The Blood Oranges*. One of the great images, one of the great moments in that novel, and I think one of the great moments in all of your fiction, is the descent into the ruined building and the discovery down in the depths of this building of a strange metal object which proves to be a chastity belt. I take it that this symbol from the past is something which seems to you very much alive in the present and is a very central image in the book, and I'm interested in how it got in there in its central position.

HAWKES: It got in there simply because when Sophie and I were in Venice we knew that a chastity belt existed in the Doge's Palace, and we set out to discover it. We ran from room to room, floor to floor, and we did discover, in light-hearted pursuit of this medieval atrocity, that the thing, when we found it, was indeed horrible. As you say, it is a central image in *The Blood Oranges*. It is central to everything I've written. That is, my fiction is generally an evocation of the nightmare or terroristic universe in which sexuality is destroyed by law, by dictum, by human perversity, by contraption, and it is this destruction of human sexuality which I have attempted to portray and confront in order to be true to human fear and to human ruthlessness, but also in part to evoke its opposite, the moment of freedom from constriction, constraint, death.

Susan Sontag

INTERVIEWED BY JOE DAVID BELLAMY

I had met Susan Sontag once, seven years before, at Antioch, where she blew great clouds of cigarette smoke above her head during her lecture describing "the new sensibility." She had nothing but scorn for American fiction of that particular moment, an unsettling message, coming from so obviously formidable a person, for my virgin ears and brain.

Author of *Against Interpretation* (1966), probably the most controversial and provocative collection of aesthetic and critical statements of the last decade in the U.S., Susan Sontag has published two novels, *The Benefactor* (1963) and *Death Kit* (1967), and a second collection of essays, *Styles of Radical Will* (1969), and she has written and directed two films, *Duet for Cannibals* and *Brother Carl*. Her stories, reviews, and essays have appeared in numerous magazines such as *Harper's Bazaar, Harper's, Partisan Review, The Nation, The New York Review of Books*, and *Commentary*.

When the opportunity for this interview presented itself, I was frankly apprehensive, remembering her Antioch appearance. But my worries were groundless; no one could have been more charming and cooperative. "I was hoping it would be you," she said, just off the plane, standing out under the awning at the arrival gate in her wraparound sheepskin collar, suede skirt, and boots, just removing a pair of blue-lens sunglasses—just that direct and unpretentious. At lunch, she laughed easily; she seemed playful, almost girlish.

During the interview, conducted later (on March 2, 1972), mostly in Mansfield, Pennsylvania, where she had come to lecture, she was a pleasure to watch—intensely serious, intellectually aggressive, sensitive, precise. The interview was completed on several pitch-black back roads that night during a long detour past rising flood waters surrounding the Chemung County airport, and it was later revised and condensed by Sontag.

JOE DAVID BELLAMY: In your essay "Against Interpretation" (1964) you said that the sense of what might be done with form in fiction written by Americans was "rudimentary, uninspired and stagnant." Do you think this is still true eight years later?

SUSAN SONTAG: No. At the time I wrote "Against Interpretation" the new American writer who interested me most was Burroughs. He was the only writer who seemed to me to have broken some of the "realist" stereotypes that limited American fiction. But since 1964 there has been a kind of explosion in prose fiction.

BELLAMY: What do you think is responsible for the new climate of the last eight years?

SONTAG: That's like asking what created the 1960s. Everything got more interesting didn't it? Look at films. Look at popular music. Even fiction, that sluggish art, couldn't resist certain influences from other arts. And there has been more sophistication, more awareness of what is going on in other places. In the immediate postwar period American writers became very provincial. In the twenties and thirties I think that American writers were much more international. Many of them spent time abroad and came in contact particularly with French literature, and writers like Joyce were very important here. But after the war there were no longer writers who were continuing even the kind of very moderate experiments of a Dos Passos or a Nathaniel West—not to mention Gertrude Stein, who was simply a figure of fun and seemed to stand totally outside American literature, or Djuna Barnes, or the still undiscovered fiction that Laura Riding wrote in the 1930s. The aims of the postwar period reverted to a kind of moral, sociological reportage in the tradition of the nineteenth century.

Then in the sixties, after I wrote that essay, people got more international again. And certain foreign writers began to have a real impact here. Borges, for instance, has mattered a lot. And older writers like Joyce, who had become college classics but who never influenced writers in the postwar period, were rediscovered.

Exactly the same thing was going on in England in that period, too, and there the novel has remained extremely conservative. A writer like Iris Murdoch was, at least at the beginning of her career, considered to be far out; and genuinely experimental writers like Virginia Woolf and Ivy Compton-Burnett had no influence whatever. What I said about American prose fiction still pretty much applies to what is going on in England—but less and less to what is happening here.

BELLAMY: Why do you think this change has come about? Is it a refusal to see reality in the same banal ways as the nineteenth-century novel saw it? A realer kind of realism? Is it the result of writers accepting the fact that thinking or fantasy is *part* of reality and is worthy of consideration (obviously that realization has an effect upon form), or is it something beyond that?

SONTAG: Partly it was the influence of other forms, I think. And partly it was the competition of other forms, like journalism, which has gotten much livelier, and TV. The form of the novel that was dominant here in that postwar period (that lasted about twenty years) was one that crystallized in the late nineteenth century before the advent of other media. But just as painting changed when photography came in, and the painter could no longer feel that his job was so self-evidently to give an image, the novel has slowly changed under pressure of tasks that are now shared in other forms.

BELLAMY: So, the novel, you would say, is having to resort to those things it can do best, those things that other forms can't do as well?

SONTAG: Well, I feel a little hesitant in talking about the novel as if it were one thing. The novels that are most popular are still in the older mold, the so-called realistic form of writing that gives what most people expect from prose fiction, a strong, clear story suggesting a certain amount of sociological and psychological information about an exotic world. The writer reports on a world you don't know: airport control towers, the Mafia, the secret life of a small town, the Hollywood movie colony, and so on.

But the relationship between more difficult fiction, which has a smaller audience, and the popular forms is still pretty close. You can see how popular fiction imitates or parodies certain formulas which began as advanced or experimental fiction. Look at the influence of Hemingway, whose stylistic mannerisms became incorporated into the most commercial kind of fiction. I think that the general public always follows the limited public, exactly as you see in the movies, where forms of film narration which only ten or fifteen years ago were to be found in avant-garde films, underground films, European art films, are now the common language of Hollywood.

BELLAMY: You see it in television too—certain film-cutting techniques.

SONTAG: And in advertising. The visual language of advertising has moved very rapidly, and has been even more directly influenced by advanced techniques from feature films.

BELLAMY: I hadn't thought about that in quite that way. I've generally been persuaded by the argument that television has influenced form in fiction, especially because of the swiftness of the image and the rapidity with which scenes and persons change. That is, even if you watch an hour series, every ten minutes you get six commercials, so you are whisked away to some faraway place. One of the conventions that seems to be growing in some experimental fiction is the use of a lot of space, a lot more space *breaks,* and that could be attributed to what is happening in television. But, of course, what's happening on television, I suppose, is either accidental or comes about from copying advanced film techniques.

SONTAG: I think it comes more from films, and that's an old influence. Faulkner and Dos Passos, for instance, were both strongly influenced by film narrative techniques, and some devices in *U.S.A.* are a direct imitation of feature film and newsreel kind of cutting. People are learning to deal with more information at the same time, and certain kinds of exposition have come to seem less necessary, even boring. Most young readers—high school and college students—will tell you that they find older novels too long. They find it hard to read Dickens or James or Tolstoy or Proust. They want something that's faster and less descriptive.

BELLAMY: Do you think the novel is headed in a new direction?

SONTAG: I think prose fiction is going to be more and more open to the influence of other media, whether that be journalism, lithography, song, or painting. It's very difficult for the novel to maintain its purity—and there's no reason why it should.

BELLAMY: Toward the end of your essay "Nathalie Sarraute and the Novel" you said you saw Sarraute's argument as basically a realist argument; that is, you point out that in getting rid of hard character and psychological explorations and the omniscient author she was actually asking for a more complex awareness of human behavior and therefore a deeper psychology and a deeper realism. Then you said that this was really a weakness in her theorizing, because the idea that the novel should approximate life is a banal idea and should be dispensed with for a while. What I'd like to ask then is: If the main purpose of the novel is *not* to imitate life, whether it's life at a fantasy or intracranial level or the level of ideas or a sociological level, what are the alternatives?

SONTAG: Intracranial?

BELLAMY: Inside of the head.

SONTAG: What isn't inside the head?

BELLAMY: Well, you know. The old epistemological distinctions —the idea of external reality as something we can all agree upon versus the idea of the individual vision which assumes that subjective reality is all there is and that yours and mine are quite different from each other.

SONTAG: I think the amount of external reality that people could actually agree on is so small, so banal, that any description involves a tremendous amount of interpretation and subjectivity. The concept of external reality as an object to be reproduced in words is very dubious. It's perfectly true that people using the same language will respond with the same words when asked to identify certain objects, certain sensory impressions. Everybody using the English language who would be considered psychologically normal would call what you're doing "sitting in a rocking chair." But there are an infinite number of ways to describe that rocking chair and you sitting in it. It's really just *naming* that we agree on, naming on a very simple level. I think the distinction between the inner and outer is not useful or interesting. And there aren't, really, any "facts." Or if there are facts, they are so primitive they're hardly worth mentioning; they're the things that everybody agrees on.

About Nathalie Sarraute—I was too hard on her. There is a real inconsistency between the theoretical program she subscribed to and what she actually was doing. But I was too severe in my emphasis on that inconsistency. So okay, she was inconsistent—because her novels are basically psychological novels. What is interesting in Sarraute is her attempt to do it all through the voice, through dialogue and inner speech and subspeech. She gives the voices one after another, what they are saying and also what they are not saying, what they are thinking. She doesn't describe how people look or what they are wearing. The method comes partly out of Joyce and also from late Virginia Woolf. *Between the Acts* is the clearest model of that kind of writing. One of the principal directions of modern literature is toward the oral, toward the recording of different kinds of human voices. The conventions of dealing with people's physical appearance that were developed through the so-called realistic novel became flat. They lost their power to enlarge people's sensibilities.

BELLAMY: All right. But still, as you are going along, it seems to me that you are adhering to a realist argument yourself. That is, you seem to be talking about the validity of finding new ways to approximate experience. You mention that Sarraute's achievement seems to be in that direction, but you also said in that essay on Sarraute that you wish the metaphor of the novel, as something that tries to approximate experience, would be retired for a while. If the novel did not try to approximate experience at some level, what else could it do?

SONTAG: I would talk in terms of creating experience. Art manipulates images that people have about their own and other people's experience, but where the notion of experience comes in, I think, is not "imitation" or "approximation" but "creation" of experience.

BELLAMY: It sounds to me as if you are describing a position that Oscar Wilde took, which was that nature imitates art. External reality is the result of the workings of our imaginations. Imagination is a faculty of perception. We make nature. That is—the inverse of Plato's notion that art copies nature.

SONTAG: Yes, I think nature imitates art more than art imitates nature, though we operate under the illusion that we are imitating nature. Artists are spokesmen of what in our sensibility is changing, and they choose among a number of possible different ways of rendering experience.

I don't think there is one way of rendering experience which is correct. I believe in a plurality of experience. I don't believe there *is* such a thing as "human experience." There are different kinds of sensibility, different kinds of demands made on art, different self-conceptions of what the artist is. And what the artist has thought it necessary to do for some time is to give people new shapes of experience, to be the cutting edge for some kind of critical or reactive change. This is hardly the only possible definition of the artist, but it's the one that has persisted in this society for well over a hundred years. The artist is someone challenging accepted notions of experience or giving people *other* information about experience or other interpretations. The artist says, "There is this cliché about this kind of experience, or this misinformation; now I will show you what it's *really* like, or I will show you *another* way of looking at it." And that is why the arts now proceed by a very rapid succession of stylistic changes, because it seems as if certain devices or forms of sensibility get used up. Once they become too widely known, too widely practiced, there is a demand for another way of looking at things. But none of this fits into any definition of art as basically realistic.

Realism is a convention. You know the marvelous book by Auerbach, *Mimesis?* What he does is examine a series of passages in which something is being described—the first is from *The Odyssey* and the last is from *Mrs. Dalloway*—to give a history of the notion of realism in European literature that spans almost three thousand years. Homer thought he was being realistic. So did Virginia Woolf. Every writer works with the idea that this is how it *really* is. Auerbach shows how the conventions of describing something have changed.

BELLAMY: Pursuing this same direction a bit further, in your essay "On Style" you said, "Every style embodies an epistemological decision, an interpretation of how and what we perceive." I take that to mean that every fiction writer makes a statement about perception and about the relationship between fiction and life. But if that's true, how can any writer escape the realist argument?

SONTAG: If *realism* is a word that applies to every writer, or at least to every writer's inner conviction about what he's doing, then it has no value at all. I think one escapes it, if you want to talk about escaping it, precisely by showing that everyone operates under the aegis of some kind of realism. Since everyone operates under it, it doesn't essentially distinguish one group of writers from another. Burroughs is as realistic as Thackeray or Arnold Bennett. It's another realism. I would never argue that people don't think they're talking about something that exists. What I was arguing against was the privileged position of a *certain* kind of realism.

BELLAMY: I think you resolved my problem.

SONTAG: When I said, "Every style embodies an epistemological decision," I didn't mean that everybody has an idea of the relation of fiction to life. I think that everybody has implicitly an idea about what is most interesting to talk about, to emphasize—because any description, any narration, any discourse, is a very radical selection of certain elements to the exclusion of many other elements. There is no total discourse. There are only partial discourses.

BELLAMY: I would like to ask you some questions about *Death Kit*—to see if there is an ideal way to understand it or what your ideal way would be. My reading of "Against Interpretation," if I may summarize that, is that you are asking for readers (or partakers of an art experience of any kind) to respond to a work of art as an aesthetic experience rather than as an intellectual experience primarily, and you complain of the tendency of criticism to push people toward an overly intellectualized response. So you want the experience of the art object to be more sensual and pleasurable and aesthetically oriented.

SONTAG: Many readers, many people who are involved in the arts as consumers, have been programmed to look for certain things in works of art—and to lie to themselves about what they actually were experiencing. They have been taught to reduce their experience to certain forms of talking about it, the most notable of these being "what it means." Confronting some art form, you say to yourself, "Well, there's this element in a painting, in a film, in a poem," and then you ask yourself, "What does it mean?" You are, in fact, changing the experience; a process of translation takes place, a false intellectualizing. But I do not view the intellectual experience as opposed to the aesthetic experience, which I felt you were doing when you reformulated my position. I think the aesthetic experience *is* a form of intelligence, and that a great deal of what people call intellectual activity is aesthetic experience.

BELLAMY: You are saying then that aesthetic experience and intellectual experience can be compatible and not necessarily at war with each other?

SONTAG: They're two parts of the same thing. And, in a sense, everything is an aesthetic experience. Our ideas about what constitute works of art have been highly conventional. We can consider anything as a work of art. Discussions go on all the time about whether to include such-and-such in the category of art or art experience. For a while, people argued about whether films were an art form. More recently there was a lot of discussion about whether the new popular music was art. This is a type of argument that goes on all the time, as certain experiences or objects are included or excluded. For instance, it's quite plausible to speak of nature as an aesthetic category. As soon as you talk about getting pleasure out of the contemplation of trees and mountains and valleys and sunsets, you're treating nature as an art work or form. There was a certain point at which people in this culture started to think of nature as beautiful—before which they didn't look at nature aesthetically. Art is that conventional area where people make objects for aesthetic consumption, and the objects are so designated in advance by the context. But anything can be put into or withdrawn from that context.

BELLAMY: What is the relation of your essays to your two novels? Do you mind if readers "interpret" your novels?

SONTAG: I wrote a series of essays between roughly 1963 and 1967—between the first novel, *The Benefactor*, and the second novel, *Death Kit*—which were based on responses which I was having as a reader, as a moviegoer, as someone moving around and coming into contact with a lot of new work that was making me rethink my own assumptions and my own tastes. Almost all those essays, as I said, were written between the first and second novel. And I don't do that kind of essay writing anymore. Unlike Nathalie Sarraute and Robbe-Grillet, I never thought that I was formulating a program for myself as a writer of fiction. I was formulating reactions and generalizations based on my experience as a reader. And I doubt that there is a very clear relation between those opinions I expressed about other people's work in literature and film and what I have done myself as a writer of fiction and as a film maker. I was not, in what I said about the novel, building an aesthetic for my own novels. I was giving my reactions as a reader. In the essays I wrote about film, I wasn't preparing the way for my own work as a film maker. I was writing as a passionate moviegoer. I feel uncomfortable when certain ideas, like the attack on one type of interpretation, are returned to me as notions which I ought to embody in my own work or as slogans which I should be reacting to in terms of what critics say about my work. I'm not against "reading," against multiple readings, against analysis.

BELLAMY: How do you feel about Theodore Solotaroff's reading of *Death Kit* in his essay "Interpreting Susan Sontag," according to which Diddy's suicide attempt in the beginning is, in fact, not an attempt but a successful suicide?

SONTAG: *Death Kit*, like *The Benefactor*, is a linear narrative which contains certain systematically obscure elements. These elements are systematically obscure because I *want* to leave several possible readings open.

BELLAMY: But could the narrative read then as the contents of his final coma?

SONTAG: Yes. One clue that supports that reading is the presence of the black orderly in the white uniform at the very beginning and at the end.

BELLAMY: So who are Hester and Incarnadona? Are they figments of his imagination?

SONTAG: Yes. In that reading this is a world of death that Diddy enters into, a fictional world in which he reprovokes his death through a series of events which he undergoes so that in the end he does die because he has collected or assembled the elements of his death. It's a second death, a second story of dying that is encapsulated through the original suicide, which was provoked by his wife leaving him.

But I like the idea that *Death Kit* can be read in that way and that it can also be read as a straight narrative in which certain magical events take place on exactly the same level as those events which are convincing in terms of everyday life.

I want the novel to have the same kind of believability that a film has. In a film, everything that you see is *there*, even if you understand that it's a flashback or it's a dream or a fantasy. Still, it fills the screen and what you see is the only reality at the moment that you see it. So, for me, it's both. It can be read in this way if you want a reading that explains how magical and conventionally realistic elements can coexist in the same life. You can say it's all a dream. But at the same time, it should be felt as an experience that was actually happening. I don't want the reader to conclude that that's what *Death Kit* is really about. I want the book to exist on both levels of reading. And it's the same for *The Benefactor*, and for the two films.

BELLAMY: Solotaroff feels that you *have* demonstrated a great deal of consistency between what you've done in this novel and your theoretical premises—as stated in your essays. He says that the "intense formalism of the novel—each detail held in place by the pattern, each event shaped by the underlying logic of Diddy's intentions—is . . . another demonstration of Miss Sontag's faith in the hegemony of form. . . ."

SONTAG: There is the same temperament in the two films and in the two novels, and there are some of the same obsessions, some of the same thematic material. Of course, I'm the same person; I'm the same sensibility. But what interests me most now is the difference between novels and films. I know that I would never have made films out of the stories of *The Benefactor* or *Death Kit*. And I would never have made novellas or novels out of the stories for *Duet for Cannibals* or *Brother Carl*. In each case, it was clear to me: that's a novel; that's a film. I'm not the kind of writer turned film maker, like Pasolini or Marguerite Duras, who can make a novel and a play and a film out of the same material.

BELLAMY: Do you think film has become the more interesting form for you then? Have you left the novel? I hope not.

SONTAG: No.

BELLAMY: Are you working now on a novel?

SONTAG: Yes. And on another film. Film is certainly the more demanding form in terms of time. You can't do it at your leisure. You work with a schedule and under considerable pressure from other people—because you can't do it alone. And then work that goes into preparing a film is very time consuming.

What interests me in each form is going beyond what I've done before. I think *Death Kit* is better than *The Benefactor* and that *Brother Carl* is better than *Duet for Cannibals.*

BELLAMY: Do you thing *Brother Carl* is better than *Death Kit* or vice versa?

SONTAG: No, I don't compare them. Both *The Benefactor* and *Death Kit* were born as language in my head. I started to hear words in my head, a tone, a voice. A certain kind of language, a certain kind of rhythm, but words—I heard words and somebody talking. In the case of *The Benefactor* it was a first-person voice. In the case of *Death Kit* it was a third-person voice, which is really a disguised first person. The two films were born as images. A film is not simply images. It is image and sound. But the first elements of the narrative I possessed were images. The dialogue seemed much less important. So perhaps the explanation of why some material becomes film and other becomes fiction is as simple as that.

BELLAMY: One observation that one might make about your fiction (and your films, too) is that if there is decipherable auto-biographical material it's more oblique than with the average writer. It's more disguised or not there. Do you think autobiographical material is irrelevant to either form, or is its absence just an accidental circumstance of your own work, or am I wrong?

SONTAG: No, you're not wrong at all. I have never been tempted to write about my own life. Most writers consciously recount and transform their own experience. But the way in which I found freedom as a writer, and then as a film maker, was to invent. Lately I have begun to think about why that's so—if it wouldn't be possible to crack this barrier. Would I be able to go someplace where I hadn't been because of it? Is it a question of inhibition or modesty or timidity? I'm not sure.

There are so many lives. All lives are possible. In the end, one does bring one's self to every character, but nothing I have written or related in film is autobiographical in the sense that it is an incident from my life.

I remember when I first started writing I wrote a long story about my best friend. I worked very hard on it, and I think it was rather good. But afterwards I felt a revulsion about the way in which I had used him, made him into an object and in that sense made myself superior to him.

BELLAMY: That's interesting because it seems just the opposite of Joyce Carol Oates's attitude. She has an amazing ability to get herself "into" people and do them, do their personalities. And her attitude is that she hopes people don't see that as vampiristic. But she feels that so many people are inarticulate and their lives need to be articulated in some way that she feels a need to do that for other people.

SONTAG: I think it is vampiristic. What would you do with your friends after you've put them in your novels? Of course, I know people don't usually resent it. I have friends who have told me with obvious pleasure that they figure in barely disguised form in novels or films. But I have a temperamental revulsion against doing that.

BELLAMY: Do you think the concept of character which comes to us from the nineteenth-century novel, that people are hardened types, is really a dangerous fallacy? We seem to be moving to a point where some writers assume that character is much more amorphous, that each person is a locus of consciousness and is much less hardened. There have even been some formal attempts to dramatize that aspect of character.

SONTAG: I think all the theories are plausible. It depends on what you do with them. There are some novels that don't have characters at all—that have different kinds of voices which you perhaps can associate with characters if you want to, but not characters in the traditional sense. There are some kinds of fiction in which people are viewed behavioristically, and there's no attempt at all to get inside them, inside what they're feeling. For instance, Borges, in his short fictions, locates people in a historical way, but there's no exploration of character. There are some kinds of fiction that work with stereotypes in which people are identified by certain exaggerated qualities they possess, and the argument of the fiction is the interplay of these different humors or types. I don't think there is any theory about character that I would want to subscribe to. The question of character: "Should character develop?" and "Is it wrong to have static or flat characters as opposed to round characters?"—the Forster distinction—is impossible to answer without a context. Either of these possibilities work.

I am most interested in kinds of fiction which are in the very broadest sense "science fiction," fiction which moves back and forth between imaginary or fantastic worlds and the so-called real world. That's what Donald Barthelme, Leonard Michaels, Ishmael Reed— many writers are doing now.

BELLAMY: How about the direction of myth—some of the things that Barth has done, or Coover?

SONTAG: If you understand the mythical allusions, then it's another level on which fiction may be pleasurable. To grasp the parallels and allusions and the play with *The Odyssey* when you read Joyce's *Ulysses* adds to your pleasure. It's another level of reading, another aesthetic game. But *Ulysses* certainly stands on its own without that knowledge. Yet it's not "better" than some other way of doing things. We live in a time of radically diversified, broken culture in which even myths are literary artifacts and not the property of people in a naïve sense. And we also live surrounded by works of art reproduced and distributed on a scale unknown since the beginning of history, where we have access to and are confronted with kinds of art of all different schools, periods, and cultures.

BELLAMY: That kind of historical burden has led some writers to end up resorting to parody.

SONTAG: Exactly.

BELLAMY: Do you see that as a valid response to the history of, let's say, fiction?

SONTAG: I think it's a dead-end response, a decadent response, that is often very creative as long as it lasts. But it can't last very long. Decadence has its pleasures and wisdom. But it's not an answer. It's a response. The glut of cultural goods creates a kind of fatigue—having too many models, too many stimuli. And parody is one way of handling the problem and copping out at the same time. If by "valid" you mean does it answer a real need, yes, it does. Its harder and harder to take things straight. Everything seems to come in quotation marks with its own built-in ironies. But I'm not sure that that situation is going to go on very long.

BELLAMY: How do you get beyond parody? What comes next? Something new? I mean, something new which is beyond anything done before? That starts to sound like an idea of progress.

SONTAG: No, I don't think there's any progress in the arts in that sense, but I think that this sort of autodestructive mechanism in the arts will come to an end, at least for a while. I don't think the arts can go on indefinitely raping themselves, eating up styles, getting more self-conscious. That's a certain period of sensibility, and people will get tired of it. There are rhythms of activity which are where people move very fast and then lie fallow for a while, and certain kinds of simplifications come to seem more desirable than that kind of sophisticated irony.

Of course, in a large part of the world all this is irrelevant. The whole discussion we've been having assumes the complicated and very privileged situation of the artist—in all forms, including the novel—in Western Europe and North America. These are special notions which prevail in societies where art is a commodity, in a kind of free market, and where the artist is rewarded even if he's a critic of his society and is some kind of outsider. There are many people in this world, in Africa, in Asia, in Latin America, who wouldn't at all agree that this is the direction of the novel or this is the problem of the artist—and who don't feel the need to parody anything and who don't worry about exhaustion and cultural glut and the relation of image and reality. It's important to remember that the discussion we're having has to do with where *we* are politically and morally, and is limited by *who* we are sociologically and historically.

Ishmael Reed

INTERVIEWED BY JOHN O'BRIEN

The fiction of Ishmael Reed doesn't conform to whatever pre-conceptions one might have about the novels of black writers, or even about American novels in general. His work just doesn't fit into convenient categories. Black critics, politicians, and the middle class are put under the knife right along with Christianity, Richard Nixon, and American history. Drawing upon techniques from such unlikely sources as vaudeville, expressionism, the narrative methods of cartoons, and the movies of Hollywood, Reed has fashioned unique fictional forms. He has satirized American culture on a great variety of subjects from the "pop" clergy of the 1960s to the Wild West. Perhaps, as an early critic claimed, he is a "revolutionary"; yes, but revolutionary in a way that few people were willing to admit a black writer could be. Reed has been planting bombs in our imaginations, disrupting our sense of what a novel should be as well as our belief about what America is. His achievement as an artist is based upon his success in discovering the style and forms that serve his satiric efforts.

The following interview was conducted in several parts between 1971 and 1973. In the winter of 1971 Reed sent me a tape filled with responses to questions I had mailed to him earlier. Over the next several months we exchanged letters. Finally, in the fall of 1973 he sent me the last tape, which responds to questions about his most recent work. In addition to his earlier novels, *The Free-Lance Pallbearers* (1967) and *Yellow Back Radio Broke-Down* (1969), Reed published—during the period of the interview—another novel, *Mumbo Jumbo* (1972), and a collection of poems, *Conjure* (1972), which were both nominated for National Book Awards. He had also been working on a collection of his own essays. Reed lives in Berkeley, California.

JOHN O'BRIEN: Can you say what the term "the new fiction" means to you? Writers like yourself, Donald Barthelme, and Charles Wright are pointed to when the term is used. Does it have any meaning to you?

ISHMAEL REED: It's obvious that there's something different when you come to the fiction of people like Clarence Major, Baraka, Wright, or Barthelme. Major was influenced by painters. Baraka was influenced by music, jazz and be-bop music. And Barthelme certainly uses a different art form in his work. I think that Wright stands alone. I think what will happen is that more writers will try to collaborate with other fields of art. Maybe this is what the new fiction is all about.

I've watched television all my life, and I think my way of editing, the speed I bring to my books, the way the plot moves, is based upon some of the television shows and cartoons I've seen, the way they edit. Look at a late movie that was made in 1947—people become bored because there was a slower tempo in those times. But now you can get a nineteenth-century 500–page book in 150 pages. You just cut off all the excess, the tedious character descriptions you get in old-fashioned prose and the elaborate scenery.

O'BRIEN: When we talked last you said that your next novel, *Mumbo Jumbo*, would be a "straight" book. I assumed that you meant it would be a return to realism. Needless to say I didn't find it conventional. It's as experimental as your first two novels. Could you explain what you meant by "straight"?

REED: When I said that it was going to be a "straight" book, I meant I would follow the classical detective story or mystery form, follow it more closely than I had the western or gothic form of my two previous novels. That's what I meant—not necessarily "straight" in style, but "straight" in form. The form is described in a headline of the *New York Times*, Monday, June 25, 1973: "Search for Suspects of Slain Policeman Provides Classic Example of Detective Work." A detective defined it as an investigation that included several lucky breaks and ingenious piecing together of seemingly unrelated bits of information. He called the investigation a "classic" example of their techniques. Many people didn't understand that I was using this detective novel form. You can have a lot of fun with this book. For example, in the 1940s the detective or mystery movies always had a form or formula where the detective would assemble all the characters involved in the crime, give a summary of how it happened, and then point to the guilty person. Well, that's what I did in *Mumbo Jumbo*, only I exaggerated. You're supposed to laugh when the detective goes all the way back to Egypt and works up to himself in reconstructing the crime. When he finishes the summary, everybody's asleep. That was meant to be humorous. I really regret that I didn't win the Edgar Allen Poe Mystery Award. I wanted to get that prize because I thought *Mumbo Jumbo* was the best mystery novel of the year.

O'BRIEN: You said before that at one point in its composition *The Free-Lance Pallbearers* seemed like a naturalistic novel but evolved into something expressionistic or surrealistic. Did *Mumbo Jumbo* undergo a similar mutation?

REED: The seed for *Mumbo Jumbo* was "D Hexorcism of Noxon D Awful," which was published in *19 Necromancers from Now* (1970) and *Amistad I*. Then I thought, "Do I want to write about the Nixon administration or do I want to transcend some particular political event and make a statement about American civilization as a whole?" As I said, the same thing happened in *Free-Lance*

Pallbearers, which began as a satire on Newark politics but expanded into a much larger universe. And this is what happened in *Mumbo Jumbo.*

I read in the paper a few weeks ago that they were reviving *King Lear* as a Watergate play. People go back into the past and get some metaphor from the past to explain the present or the future. I call this "necromancy," because that's what it is. People have challenged me on the use of the word, but that's just because they don't think niggers should use words over three or four syllables. But I know what I'm talking about. Necromancers used to lie in the guts of the dead or in tombs to receive visions of the future. That is prophecy. The black writer lies in the guts of old America, making readings about the future. That's what I wanted to do in *Mumbo Jumbo.*

When I first did the satire on Nixon everybody in New York was down on me. Kate Millett and I were at a party at Florence Kennedy's house. Somebody remarked about Nixon being successful. And at this time in 1969 Nixon was successful—he was going to end the war. They asked how I could write this kind of thing. But I always look at the pattern and the personality. I think if you look at Nixon you can explain American civilization. The American people elected him and this must say something about them. He comes from a small town, Whittier, California, a small town with its ghost stories and superstitions, home-spun recipes, ethnic rivalries, primitive nationalism, and primitive racism. Whittier, California, could be DeKalb, Illinois, or it could be the Hudson River valley that Washington Irving wrote about. I told them at the party that you have to look at the pattern of a man. I said that Nixon's a loser, and, if he wins, his victory is just building up for a bigger loss.

So, I decided that I didn't want to use the King Lear model because that's someone else's experience. I didn't want to invoke Antigone as the French did to talk about Hitler. I want to go into the mysteries of the American civilization. The American civilization has finally got its rhythm; looking into the past you can see the rhythms of this civilization. So I stepped back to an age that reminds me of the one I'm writing in. I stepped back to the twenties. Instead of Nixon I invoked Harding. The parallels between the two are remarkable. I was reading *The Harding Era* by Murray the other night, and there are obvious parallels. For instance, future president Herbert Hoover tried to warn Harding that the Tea Pot Dome scandal was getting out of hand and that he ought to make a full revelation of it. There was a burning of papers in the Harding affair. Harding got pneumonia. The people around him who stole were amateurs. A lot of parallels.

But I began *Mumbo Jumbo* long before the Watergate scandal, although it's interesting that in the book I have a photograph that includes, from right to left, John Mitchell, Richard Kleindienst, and behind, if you look closely enough, John Dean. I had no idea that the Watergate thing was about to break when I used this picture. The book was submitted to Doubleday in April, 1971. But I have this picture of these people looking down on the Yippies doing a May dance in the street. I have the picture in the book because I try to use all the patterns of the time. For example, the great conspiratorial thing of the sixties—there was always a conspiracy seen behind political events—well, I exaggerate that, so that I have the Knights Templar in rivalry with the followers of Jes Grew, which dates back to Osiris. And I have the picture there. It's necromancy. You try to prophesy; you get strange feelings or impulses. I do believe that I get psychic information from sources I'm not even aware of when I'm writing. That's prophecy. But that's only one element of the book. I took all these things, used the classic techniques of the detective novel, as well as Egyptology, Western history, black dance, American civilization, and the Harding administration—all myths to explain the present. I think I was right on target. I'm very pleased with the way events are working out—on one level.

O'BRIEN: Then the artist and the prophet have a common vocation?

REED: That is what the artist does. He still has his role in prophecy. I told a conference the other day that Jean Dixon and I are in the same ball park, except that she's a realist.

O'BRIEN: And *Mumbo Jumbo* is antirealistic?

REED: Of course the book has all kinds of styles. There are naturalistic passages and there are some which are not naturalistic. There are some passages which do what painters do, using peripheral information to explain an event, meshing the factual and the imaginative.

O'BRIEN: How do the factual and the imaginative relate to one another? Do you try to reflect what is real, or, through the imagination, do you create new realities?

REED: Both. I recall a good example of art creating reality. We've seen in the twentieth century political movements that were begun by artists who were brought into the streets. The Black Panthers came out of a theater movement in San Francisco. Cultural people like Ed Bullins kept it on the stage while the political "actors" took it out into the streets. They were able to convince the administration in Washington that they had some gigantic movement. Even though I criticized some of these activities, I think that this is an extremely sophisticated form of drama that they were acting out. I think that Baraka said he had brought things off the stage and into the streets. In this situation theater influenced reality. Art influenced politics. These fifty "actors" demonstrated and exaggerated, as actors do, and convinced the Nixon administration that there were thousands and thousands of Black Panthers surrounding them. They had to put covered wagons around the White House, which is also a theater. Often reality is art.

I remember in the early sixties the newspapers came out with "The long, hot summer, the long, hot summer." They kept saying it over and over again, and finally the long, hot summer occurred. If these few actors are responsible for exposing the fascism that has come into government in the last twenty years and have helped in the government being meticulously reviewed, then they were successful as artists. It works both ways—art can reflect and create reality.

O'BRIEN: Do you have any insights on why *Mumbo Jumbo* enjoyed such a wide critical success, especially in New York, which was denied to your first two novels? Has something changed among the critics in the last few years? I have in mind the front-page review in the *New York Times*.

REED: A lot of things have changed. When we talked last Francis Brown was the editor of the *New York Times Book Review*. He was described as a "Tory" by some people. I don't think he's very sympathetic to contemporary experimental literature. Now you have John Leonard. He's more amenable to what's happening in contemporary American writing. From time to time he writes articles disapproving of so-called experimental literature, but at least he recognizes its existence. I think this is what has changed in the *New York Times*. I don't know how they arrive at the decision about what's to be reviewed up front. I have no idea how things are decided. I live in Berkeley. Unfortunately, New York is a cultural center—and there are many historical reasons for this. It has cultural vitality because it is a melting pot.

O'BRIEN: Then the old literary establishment which you talked about a few years ago is tottering?

REED: I don't think I talked about the literary establishment as a monolith. I talked about individuals in the literary establishment. We still have problems from black and white ideologists. On the white side there is what I would call "The Irving Howe School of Critics on Black Writing." Morris Dickstein and people like that are in this school. It's very interesting that the Jewish tradition in American writing begins in 1900 and the black tradition begins about the middle of the eighteenth century. We've been here longer than they have. But they become the experts on our literature and culture for some reason which I haven't yet been able to figure out.

You can always get the tip-off that they are trying to use black literature to make some kind of thesis when they begin their surveys with Richard Wright. They all begin with Richard Wright. That's like beginning a survey of white American literature with Norman Mailer instead of with Cooper, Brown, or Hawthorne.

That's how you can see that they haven't done careful research on the field. They use it for rather dubious ends. And they never mention Richard Wright's later work, like *The Outsider* and the things he wrote in Europe. They take *Native Son*, for obvious reasons. They use black literature to make a political statement. These people are socialists. And blacks do the same thing.

O'BRIEN: Some black critics are just as doctrinaire and restrictive as the white liberal critics?

REED: When you talk about "black," you're being superficial. Caste and class enter into it. If you look at Reconstruction, you'll find that many high yellows took advantage of its opportunities. Every time a Negro mania sweeps the country, which happens from time to time, where people adopt black art forms and culture, fashion and talk, the high yellows usually take advantage of this. For example, in the 1960s black poetry was begun by darker-skinned people; in the mid-sixties high yellows took it over because high yellows make it more palatable to the white establishment; after all, they are their children. A lot of high yellow people use blackness. I wouldn't bring this up if it were not a fact, but it is a fact. The high yellows exploit blackness while still using their skin privileges. The slave master is always going to look out for his kids, even though he once sold them. He's always going to look out for his kids before he looks out for darker-skinned people. So we have high yellows who all of a sudden discovered Malcolm X last week and have had a nervous breakdown every day since then. They start an extortion racket on blackness and black writers. So you get it from both sides.

O'BRIEN: But one of the racial myths in America is that divisions of this kind among blacks do not exist. The popular media talk about "black leaders" or "black spokesmen." With whites, however, it's always in terms of liberals or conservatives, Republicans or Democrats. No one would know what a "white spokesman" is.

REED: The black male in this country cannot talk about all the aspects of his oppression. If I say that the white establishment or the power structure is oppressing me, I can get away with it. But if

I say that blacks are oppressing me, even if I give evidence of how I'm oppressed by other blacks, I get censored. I'm getting more and more interested in slavery as a metaphor for how blacks are treated in this civilization. We have the same old lineup. The Irving Howe crowd and the liberals in New York are the abolitionists.

I remember an old abolitionist poster in a Langston Hughes book on black history. The poster said that we have to help niggers because they can't speak for themselves. They're helpless. That attitude is still here. And we have the high yellows, the slave master's children, who want to keep you in line and secretly despise you. We have the overseer; we have the whole classical plantation tradition. So I say to myself and the rest of us that we are going to get to our aesthetic Canada, no matter how many dogs they send after us. We'll get there. I'm in my tradition and they can be in theirs.

I think it a good sign that there are more and more critics, both black and white, who are looking at the whole field objectively instead of writing the classical oppressive criticism that blacks have received in this country. So the white liberal school of critics is receding because you have better critics replacing them.

O'BRIEN: How is this oppression from blacks manifested?

REED: Some of those people who call themselves nationalists and revolutionaries are your worst enemies because, in many ways, they're sicker than the mainline critic who's a superficial expert on blackness. You get those blacks who feel that just because you're the same skin color . . . shit! most of the time I'm cherry red. I'm beginning to see why black writers flee this country.

I can see how difficult the writers in the past had it who were independent—people like George Schuyler, Chester Himes, and a contemporary like John Williams. The "saving grace" is that there are more independent writers around now who are not going to stand for this extortion. We're not masochists. I'm not a masochist. We're not into self-flagellation. I'm not a Christian. This is a big battle; it's the most interesting cultural development in Afro-American history. We will end the situation in which people like Hugh Hefner can secretly finance and put fascism on us.

O'Brien: Doesn't such independence interfere with the official crowning of *the* black writer of the decade? First there was Wright, then Ellison, then Baldwin. Who can it be in the seventies?

Reed: There's always a seat up for grabs, and every faction in the establishment has its token darkie. What happened was that Baraka (LeRoi Jones) courageously walked away from it; Calvin Hernton walked away from it. You're supposed to stay in New York when your book is published and be exploited. Calvin Hernton went to England. I left New York before my book came out because I wanted to make it on the merit of the book and not on the merit of playing tennis with George Plimpton or being at Town Hall with some liberal. We're confusing the picture. Crazy niggers! You've got the rise of the crazy niggers. Crazy means a "wit." In Zora Hurston's book *Dust Tracks on a Road* "crazy" means "witty." That's what proletariat black people mean when they say "crazy nigger." So, we're messing up the script. But you've always got these liberals grooming people. They always want a token spokesman whom they can use for talking "android," as I said in *Mumbo Jumbo*. Now they have this poor guy (I won't mention his name) who's been appointed the successor to Baldwin. (But Baldwin's in good shape—re-read *Tell Me How Long the Train's Been Gone*— he's in very good shape. Nobody's going to take his seat.) But Ralph Ellison and Irving Howe told him he's the best one, and all the rest of us are into rhetoric. He called me up when *Mumbo Jumbo* got such a great critical reception and gave me the reasons why it was so well received—none of the reasons had to do with merit. But we're confusing the picture and it's more difficult for them to point to any particular Afro-American writer as being the "one," which is the way it was done historically.

In the twenties you got this, too. Why do we hear more about Langston Hughes than we do about Rudolph Fisher, Wallace Thurman, and George Schuyler? It's a very interesting question, and the critics ought to go into it.

O'Brien: So far I have limited myself to asking you about the innovations you have made in fiction. I wonder whether you think you write "conventional" essays. I admit that I have read only a few, but it seems to me that they are alogical and that, in place of logic, you depend upon perceptions which you do not weigh down with cumbersome arguments. I suspect that your approach to fiction and essay writing may be somewhat the same. Just as you avoid detailed character descriptions, settings, and all of the other trappings of realistic fiction, you also seem to avoid classical rhetorical devices in your essays.

REED: We know from the history of logic that logic doesn't necessarily have anything to do with truth. From my classroom experience I know that the old scholastic philosophers used to cheat on their syllogisms concerning the existence of God. In the first premise it was hidden that God existed anyway; then they went on to prove what they had already posited. I write essays on the basis of feeling. That's why I published one of them in a book of poetry, because it's more in the realm of poetry than the classical essay with "all its rhetorical devices." Of course, a great deal of truth has come out this way. A lot of scientific conclusions that we live with today were based upon hunches and intuitions written in what we consider a "wild" way.

The Sufi Muslims have an essay style called "scatter," in which people go from one subject to another—which is what I do. That's the way my mind works. I'll go into one topic and then go into its ramifications. Sometimes I lose where I started from. It's the Afro-American writer who's asked to have all the facts and arguments. But facts and arguments haven't gotten him anywhere. They can prove things forever, but most people live on the basis of the irrational.

I'm reading Wilhelm Reich's *The Mass Psychology of Fascism*. I can see why you would jail a man like that. People go through life considering themselves normal, believing they act in a logical way. Then all of a sudden somebody comes along who is able to draw upon some dark urge or primitive instinct and capture their imaginations. . . . Some of my friends talk about the "system"—that they're fighting the system. There's no system in America. If the economists in Washington knew what they were doing, you wouldn't have the crisis you have now. This is really one of the most romantic governments ever. You never know what's going to happen next.

But it depends upon the kind of essay I'm writing. In a book review for mass publication I write "straight" prose pieces.

Norman Mailer can say in his book *Marilyn* that Marilyn Monroe had a crush on Clark Gable because he reminded her of her father —a father complex. That's certainly wild speculation. She might have been interested in Clark Gable because he had a mustache and she had some big thing about hair. Your guess is as good as mine. But it's always the black writer who's accused of rhetoric if he makes some wild hypothesis. When a white writer indulges in wild hypotheses they call him a genius.

O'BRIEN: Do you think that fiction has a future? The novel-is-dead critics made their autopsy several years ago, but the novel seems reluctant to rest in peace.

REED: One trend I see now is that you are going to get other ethnic groups into the ballgame. I'm interested in what the Asians out here in California are doing. They combine their experience with that of other ethnic groups. A person like Frank Chin is influenced by black and white culture but in addition has an identity of his own. That engenders a hybrid that really fascinates and amazes me.

The novel-is-dead idea is probably something created by businessmen who are more interested in pushing books that sell, books about how to do things or how to diet. Storytelling will always exist. You'll have other people writing, different groups, and maybe they'll create their establishments. You'll get more independent publishing companies, more controlled by artists and writers. Small publishers. Literature will be kept alive and will endure.

Jerzy Kosinski

INTERVIEWED BY JEROME KLINKOWITZ

"His art has dealt with the fangs and colors of dream and of daily life among the violations of the spirit and body of human beings." So read the statement of the National Institute of Arts and Letters when it granted Jerzy Kosinski an award "for creative work in literature," just before the publication of his third novel, *Being There*, in 1970. Kosinski is among the more widely honored American novelists writing today, winning the Prix du Meilleur Livre Etranger for his first fictional work, *The Painted Bird* (1965), and the National Book Award for *Steps* (1968).

We cannot know how close Kosinski was to the wartime horrors of *The Painted Bird* or the transitional agonies of *Steps*, although the themes of those novels, of *Being There*, and of the book he was completing when our interview took place (*The Devil Tree*, 1973) center philosophically on "the self." Reviewers sense the problem and make the most of it, as when John Updike, careful as always about a book's design, noted that the typography of *Being There* "suggests that Kosinski's biography is the last chapter." His life does present a high profile: the professorships, awards, and degrees, but also the exposure as a talk show personality, as world traveler while the husband of a steel heiress (now deceased), and even as a late-comer to a party he could not have regretted missing, at the home of his close friends Roman Polanski and Sharon Tate on August 8, 1969. But besides the public record of his own self, Kosinski has studied the role of selves in modern life, not simply as a novelist but originally as a professor of sociology. It was to have been his career in Poland, where after a chaotic and catastrophic childhood (which left him mute and illiterate into his teens) he quickly approached the top of academia, earning graduate degrees in history and political science and undertaking as his special interest the self in collectivized society. Two of his scholarly works were published in Poland, and after his dramatic emigration to America in 1957 at the age of twenty-four he drew on notes for a third to produce *The Future Is Ours, Comrade* (1960) and *No Third Path* (1962), written under the pseudonym of "Joseph Novak."

Jerzy Kosinski invited me to meet him at Yale University in November of 1971—a few weeks earlier than originally planned; the night before (Halloween) I'd seen his friend Roman Polanski's *Repulsion* for the first time and was still reeling in nightmares when Kosinski's morning phone call summoned me from Chicago to New Haven. With books and notecards and personal emotions all in great disarray, I arrived at Kosinski's residence in Davenport College late Sunday evening and was met with a graciousness and candor which made a solid eight hours' conversation (four that night, four the next morning) possible. Kosinski's presence is commanding: physically tall, thin, and of intense personal bearing, he impresses one with his great range of knowledge and personal experience. Yet my own comfort seemed foremost in his mind, and the contagion of this attitude (plus a healthy supply of Heineken's Light) moved us into a good talk about his literary achievement.

Our most substantial discussions centered on his theory of writing and how he followed the involved course of moving from sociological study (in Polish) through award-winning international photography to his current success as a novelist writing exclusively in his adopted language, English. Since *The Devil Tree* was then in progress, I have omitted the few references he made to it in favor of Daniel J. Cahill's interview with Kosinski (*North American Review*, Spring, 1973), which is devoted exclusively to this latest work.

JEROME KLINKOWITZ: Many people would like to ask you, I suppose, whether all those incidents in *The Painted Bird* "really happened to you." I won't ask that, but you did tell Cleveland Amory [*Saturday Review*, April 17, 1971, p. 16] that during World War II you were separated from your family.

JERZY KOSINSKI: Yes.

KLINKOWITZ: Was it really for a period as long as in the book, six years, that you were on your own?

KOSINSKI: Yes. From 1939 until 1945. But I was mute for a longer time than was the Boy in *The Painted Bird*. He's mute for about three years, from 1942, let's say, to the end of 1945, when he regains his speech. I was mute from 1942 until 1948, more than six years.

KLINKOWITZ: At what stage did you begin your formal education, such as learning to read?

KOSINSKI: Formal education? Kindergarten before the war. Then, at the age of twelve, as a mute in the special school (1945–1947); and then two years later I was transferred, still mute, to be taught to write and to read by my father and privately hired tutors. When I got my speech back (1948) I went directly to the Gymnasium and Lyceum of Humanities.

KLINKOWITZ: The first edition of *The Painted Bird* closes with an italicized postscript I don't find in subsequent editions.

KOSINSKI: The postscript resulted from a mistake. Initially in my correspondence with the publisher I often defended the idea of the book. In one letter I speculated about the "future" of the novel's protagonist, about the fate of the Boy "after the War." I wrote this letter from Europe where I was traveling. The editor at Houghton Mifflin thought that this was a "very telling letter," and she also thought that it could—indeed, should—become a postscript to *The Painted Bird*, and apparently she cabled me about it; since the final galleys were just about to be sent to the printers, she rushed and used the negative option: if I would not reply she would assume that I agreed. Well, I was in France, staying in a large, disorganized hotel, and I never received that cable. Sometime later the book was published with that italicized ending. Unlike this unintended "epilogue" there were, however, many well-intended passages, paragraphs, and phrases of the original manuscript which did not make their way to Houghton's edition of *The Painted Bird*; even though they appeared in the final corrected galley proofs they were dropped "in the last minute"; we had an argument about it. All omitted parts were reintroduced in the Pocket Book edition [1966], to the revised Modern Library edition [1970], and to the forthcoming Bantam Book 1972 edition.

KLINKOWITZ: That very postscript suggests, of course, more of your own experience, particularly the Stalinization of Poland and the introduction of a collectivized society, which you subsequently studied and wrote about in *The Future Is Ours, Comrade* and *No Third Path*. I am intrigued by how your career developed from these roots—how you moved from sociology to photography and finally to fictional art.

KOSINSKI: First, when I saw myself as a sociologist, as a social scientist, I assumed that I was already operating on a high level of abstraction. Indeed, equal to that of fiction; after all, a sociologist abstracts certain social forces into meaningful formulas which could be perceived by others in an act of self-recognition. During the Stalinist period I became aware that this was not possible, that being a sociologist I was not only writing fiction, but that "the plot" of my "fiction" was given to me by the very forces which I resented and abhorred and was terrified by—the Communist party and its totalitarian system. Of course, I realized that as a social scientist I was not at all a writer of "sociological fiction," so to speak, but that I was writing a script for Stalinist policemen, who might use my abstract script to arrest living people. My sociological dissertation would be used as a program for a pogrom, as any other piece of social writing would be used. Or, if I refused to make it politically "valid," it would be used as a program for a pogrom of me, of my family, and of my friends. Hence, I began moving towards chemistry.

To make this sudden new interest legitimate I enrolled as an auditor in the courses in photographic chemistry; otherwise, abandoning Marxism and Leninism for the sake of black-and-white photography would be considered a political act of antisocialist character. Later, as if by accident, I began taking pictures as well as developing them—my first black-and-white photographs had a very good reception by the official photographers of the Soviet Union and—later, in Poland also—and I became a member of the photographers' union; I was officially allowed to practice photography; I received access to the university's darkroom. Then I received an official permission to read Western photographic books, magazines, and catalogs which were kept in a restricted part of the university library. Several of my better photographs I submitted to various national and then international exhibitions of photography; some of them won prizes. By 1957 my photographs were exhibited at more international exhibitions than anybody else's in Eastern Europe. And so I moved even further away from language.

The photographic darkroom became a symbol of my life. Only in the darkroom I could function without being watched. While safely locked inside there, I would turn the lights on; then I could read from time to time some of the forbidden literary works, but not that many—I was too careful, and after all, the darkroom was used by many people, and since anyone could be accused of having brought these books inside, I would bring them with me carefully packed inside photographic paper ("sensitive to light—open only in the darkroom"—how appropriate!). That was frightening, frankly. I didn't read much. I managed to get some volumes of Nietzsche in Polish prewar translation. I read some of Dostoyevsky, which was not readily available, but I could always claim that, after all, Dostoyevsky was published by the Soviet publishers, so my crime was not that great. Nevertheless, photography became my ultimate interest at the time, and I felt that becoming a professional photographer was the best thing I could do as long as I was in Poland or in the U.S.S.R.

But I wanted to escape, and I embarked on a very long and complex process of preparing my escape, a process which took me almost two years. In my scheme I had to literally invent people who would sponsor me in my actual departure from Poland. Since I would be leaving my parents, my adopted brother, and some of my friends behind, I wouldn't want anyone to be responsible for my escaping. Hence *I had to* invent people of authority. Only they could help me; I could trust them. They couldn't be blamed; their families couldn't be arrested. Within the totalitarian bureaucratic jungle it was not that difficult to invent a few additional bureaucratic animals; the jungle would absorb them readily. And I invented four eminent scholars, all highly placed in the academic hierarchy, who sponsored my departure. Three of them were in favor of my departure; one was against my leaving Poland. Even though this was for the sake of plausibility, I didn't like him, I remember, and I had some difficulty writing critical letters which "he" had to write about me, so to speak, since in these letters I had to produce some authentic negative aspects of my personality. I remember resentment I felt towards *his* correspondence, and great apprehension towards the answers he was receiving from other, real, bureaucrats about me, particularly from those who had agreed with him and who volunteered negative opinions of their own. The other three kept writing basically in my favor—three to one in my favor! Not bad in a police state.

Only after I arrived in the United States I realized that my interest was not photography; even though I had my cameras with me and could have accepted various jobs as a photographer, I refused to do so. I felt that I had to concentrate on language; I had to acquire language as quickly as possible. Not only for the purpose of speaking (this even today is not my prime interest), but for expressing myself in writing. Now a darkroom became a writing desk, and paper remained sensitive to light, but in a different way. I, not the manufacturer, would make it sensitive, and I would make it sensitive by the inking I would place on its surface. As a photographer I knew that the basic purpose of the photographic process was to reproduce the reality and that photography would actually accomplish it. If there was a tree in the field and I photographed and developed it in my darkroom, I actually could do this so it would match exactly the imaginary photograph in my mind. Well, I found this profoundly distressing. If my imagination was able to conceive of the images which could be so easily reproduced in the Soviet darkroom—in any darkroom—then clearly there was not much to my imagination. I found it very humiliating that in a photograph I actually could produce what I thought.

With writing I can only approximate the vision I have. I can only encode it, and by encoding I'm sending a cable through an abstract messenger to an unknown receptor. I don't know whether it will be read or who will read it and what it will mean to him. And this *not knowing*—it's exactly what I cherish in writing novels, since I'm basically concerned with *my* imagination and with *my* encoding; not with anything else, not with anyone else. I assume that my using the language connects me and my readers— whoever they are—in the most profound of ways, but I'm not giving my reader every detail of black and white, or of Kodacolor, with all the shadows in between. I am merely pointing out the tree in the field. Whether my reader will "see" the field or a tree or my intent to show them in a certain manner is something I will never know. How he will see it and what it will mean to him will remain, for me, a mystery. This is why I think I would never be able to go back to visual arts of any kind; even if I would write nothing but telephone books and list names and phone numbers, they would still have for me greater evocative power than the best of my photographs.

KLINKOWITZ: At times in the books on collective behavior you do present images almost as a novelist would. In *The Future Is Ours, Comrade* there's one incident in which you had a shop window where there were all sorts of goods, radios, appliances, and there were the pictures of the party leaders among them.

KOSINSKI: In *No Third Path* you might have noticed the metaphor of the painted bird. That is when the embryo of my idea of the book was born.

KLINKOWITZ: And in *No Third Path* there are dramatic scenes, where the interviewer talks to an old man in the park, a little child comes rushing up and is scared away; this seemed to me more literary art than detached sociology.

KOSINSKI: I don't think that there is a detached sociology. It is merely another form of encoding; perhaps a different form of literary fiction.

KLINKOWITZ: So many incidents from these two books appear later in your fiction: the "painted bird," as you mentioned, the Soviet officer Gavrila (whom you visit as an old friend in *No Third Path* and who appears in *The Painted Bird* as the officer who adopts the Boy), the wrestler in the concentration camp, and even the character who, in the collective state, can find privacy in lavatories. Would you contrast the different uses made of similar incidents in the fiction books with the nonfiction?

KOSINSKI: The difference is that my nonfiction grounds it in a specific place—the U.S.S.R.—and by doing so torpedoes its immediacy, its proximity to the reader. On the other hand, the fiction invokes the reader directly. He cannot discard it by saying, "It already happened to someone else, hence it won't happen to me. I'm excluded; I'm a bystander." Perhaps the "nonfiction as literature" aims at nonevoking; it aims at reassuring the reader that the event had taken place or that it's a large historical process, hence that there's no direct threat to the reader. Fiction assaults the reader directly as if saying: It is about you. You are actually creating this situation when you are reading about it; in a way you are staging it as an event of your own life.

KLINKOWITZ: You mentioned once on *The Tonight Show* that as a friendless young immigrant in the United States you would

sometimes call telephone operators to help you with matters of
stylistics for your first book in English (*The Future Is Ours, Comrade*).

KOSINSKI: Well, not quite. I did not expect telephone operators
to help me in matter of style. It was a problem of simple communi-
cation. Knowing no one who could "play back" the idea which
I tried to express in written English, it occurred to me that in the
middle of the night in New York there was, after all, a person who
was available, a voice which would answer, and who would have
to perceive my images only through the words.

In other words, the level of abstraction was maintained; *I* would
not be seen; my gestures would not "be read"; *I* would use only
the sound of the language. Thus, I would call a New York telephone operator and I would describe my predicament. I would
tell her that I was a foreigner, that I was writing a scholarly work
in a recently adopted tongue, and that since some of the passages
of this work described situations not commonly known in the
United States, I wanted to make certain that they would be understood and that she understood them. Then I would read a passage
describing, let's say, a multifamily apartment in the Soviet Union,
in which people would use one common bathroom and kitchen,
and so forth, and I would ask her: Did she understand the paragraph? How would she see these people? Could she now tell what
it all meant to her? This was a simple case of finding a potential
reader, so to speak. . . . Very often a telephone operator would
say "I'm not sure I understand it. What do you mean that everyone
would use the same kitchen? Would this mean that they all had
their own utensils? Or would they share the same towels?" Good
questions. I was asked, "When they use the same bathroom do they
bring their own things with them each time they go to the
bathroom? . . ."

In *The Future Is Ours* when I would say that the Russians find
their privacy on the street this came as a great shock to the telephone
operators, who couldn't see how any privacy could be found in the

street. Hence, in the book, I had to illustrate a bit more, by making a point that unlike Americans who are pleased with changes in their immediate surroundings, in things they own—a better car, newer furniture, a bigger house—Russians often find pleasing change in the way the street is "furnished"—a new building, a new monument, a new traffic system—all the embroidery which the government creates for the street, which of course to the citizens typifies the progress. This was the initial stage of my writing of the book: I looked for an ideal reader. I dialed "O."

KLINKOWITZ: But it had nothing to do with language itself.

KOSINSKI: Nothing to do with language as structure, as style. Of course not. I had access to all the grammars I wanted and to all the dictionaries I needed, and I had maintained a very elaborate correspondence with my father which runs into almost 2,000 sheets, three letters a week, dealing only with the English usage. My father was a philologist—he knew English quite well. With his help I was well equipped to use the dictionaries, the synonym finders, the word finders, the grammar manuals. I couldn't speak, of course. I had great difficulty explaining to the telephone operator what I wanted from her; I would have to write it first for myself—a little screenplay, almost—and read it to her so she would know what I expected of her. Very often my foreign accent interfered, and some telephone operators were not quite certain what was actually the word I used. There was no one else I could really do these tests with, since during the day I worked as a truck driver.

KLINKOWITZ: You wrote *The Future* in 1959–1960—it was published in 1960. This is a bare three years after you'd arrived. . . .

KOSINSKI: Actually I arrived in December, 1957; the book was published in May, 1960.

KLINKOWITZ: So two and a half years. I'm just wondering at what point do you feel you really gained a facility with English?

KOSINSKI: In terms of writing? Or in terms of speaking?

KLINKOWITZ: In terms of writing.

KOSINSKI: In terms of writing, I would think about nine months after I arrived, but this has been a never-ending process. In terms of speaking, about a year and a half later, but I am still working at it. No prison is as impregnable as that of language.

KLINKOWITZ: In the Dutch edition of your collected essays[1] you add a statement that writing in an adopted language offers you "one more curtain that separates [you] from spontaneous [and hence uncontrolled] expression." Does this mean that raw experience cannot spill over into your work—that it must be refined by some artistic process?

KOSINSKI: Well, yes. I think language is both a maze and a veil. I think all men perceive themselves and their environment in a verbalized form; by comparison with a man who speaks the step-mother's tongue, a native perceives his reality in a perhaps less organized way. His consciousness of the "form" of his language seems to be of a slightly diluted character. Perhaps he remains more emotional, more spontaneous, and less aware of the censorious processes which language imposes on him. He might not fully realize that his emotions have been fitted already into the molds of the language. Hence, in my view, a "lower-class" experience is different from the "upper-class" not only in terms of the content of the actual experience but in terms of its organization, its ordering by language at the time when it had occurred. For instance, a peasant does not perceive his reality as brutal. However, his language transcribed and read by the middle class indicates brutalizing experience, since it is perceived in a different fashion.

Now, conversely, if this is the case, then something else also is taking place. Language connects us not only with our primary reality, with the reality of the self, with the reality of the emotion; it also connects us with a certain social reality outside us. Language becomes the connective link. One is traumatized by the language when one is growing up. In our society the adults use the language as a reprimanding device. A child often cannot help feeling

1. *Tijd van leven—tijd van kunst* [Time of life—time of art] (Amsterdam: Uitgeverij de Bezige Bij, 1970). Originally published as *Notes of the Author* and *Art of the Self* (New York: Scientia-Factum, 1965 and 1968).

that certain words hurt just as much as certain gestures do. A native, because of this, is at the same time more idiosyncratic to certain aspects of his language, of his self, than a foreign-born writer who adopted a new language long after his formative years. One can ask which are the formative years. I think had I come to the United States at the age of nine I would have become affected by this traumatizing power of language. At the age of seventeen it would have been too late. When I came to the United States I was twenty-four.

Hence, I am not traumatized by my English—no part of my English affects me more or less than any other one. For instance, a writer who writes in his native tongue may feel emotionally uneasy about using vernacular even when he knows why he is uneasy about using vernacular. When manipulating the language a native writer faces many conflicts. Even though he remains spontaneous he avoids certain language, exposes another, and his creative choices are determined to a great degree by his adolescence and by his childhood—by the period of his initial entry into the language, into the very language which orders experience.

Now, a man who at the age of twenty-four, for example, arrives in a new country with an entirely different set of encoding—emotional encoding stemming from another language—in the beginning finds himself in a vacuum. His language makes no sense in the new environment, and the language of the new environment evokes nothing in him. However, once the newcomer masters the new language he discovers two sets of responses within him. One to his native tongue, which he might classify as an adolescent response. It is the immediate response which evokes almost uncontrollable reflexes, particularly towards the vernacular, the language of reprimand, the language of abuse, etc. Another response is almost nonemotional, and it is caused by his acquired stepmother's tongue, which doesn't have the ability to traumatize. No matter how well you know this tongue (providing you did not grow "in it") and how well you manipulate it, it lacks the edge of spontaneous reflex. Hence, a foreigner, one could claim, has certain emotional advantage in the new language he has chosen to use. It

won't traumatize him easily. For instance, in the U.S.A. my fear of
bureaucratic language, my fear of the language of the law, is "intellectual"; there is no emotion which similar Polish or Russian
language evokes in me.

KLINKOWITZ: Are you saying that the foreigner is in control of
his stepmother language, while in his mother language he is more
determined?

KOSINSKI: Perhaps one could claim the paradoxical: that a native
is less in control of the language. The language controls him.

KLINKOWITZ: Is it the foreigner's practice, then, that makes great
art? Or even art per se, as opposed to a native speaker working
purely out of experience, which, when we trace back, we see he's
really not in control of?

KOSINSKI: I think this differs from writer to writer. What is the
function of literature? What makes literature? I think those who
write and who think about what and how they write have their own
answers. I thought about it simply because I wanted to find out
exactly what is the actual prompting which makes me do what
I do, particularly what are the promptings which *prevent* me from
doing what I want to do very often. I know there are certain areas
of the Polish or Russian or English language which touch me
emotionally more than others. And maybe because of my awareness of the English language imposed on me by circumstances since
I was twenty-four, I have adopted an outlook which I might never
have acquired had I decided to write in my own language. And
maybe that's why I have never written anything creative in my
own language. Maybe that's why I would never have considered
to write anything in Polish or in Russian (I was bilingual). I think
that a foreign-born writer who manipulates the adopted language
(as opposed to the native who is more manipulated by the language) more consciously selects from "the verbal environment" its
pivotal aspects.

For a foreigner writing in an adopted tongue, the act of perception is edited already; it means that if I am aware of the new language and if I am also aware of the process of editing which had

already taken place, I might as well carry it to a very definite conclusion.

A man who returns home and tells about an accident cannot
possibly convey *all* of the accident—allness is simply not conveyable.
He has to select what he considers the crucial ingredients, the most
pregnant symbols. He doesn't bring slides, after all, or photographs.
He must select certain basic ingredients out of "the vocabulary of
an accident," assuming that those he will tell it to will supply their
imagination and their knowledge of accidents as well; that he
will thus tap *existing* knowledge about accidents—their imaginary
knowledge—the cultural knowledge—which will make his experience conveyable to them. You could certainly use all of the large
Oxford dictionary, all 450,000 words, to describe one accident. You
still could have run out of words. Then you'd perhaps use some
French. And some German.

It follows, then, that a novelist cannot aim at conveying the most.
He fits his language into the preexisting body of imagination in
such a way that his language prompts those who are "on the receiving end" to provide the rest since they clearly *can* provide the
rest. They embody the collective experience of "an accident." (Unless, of course, one would want to communicate with people from
an entirely different realm of cultural experience.)

You asked me before how a writer selects "the bare minimum."
I think there's no predictable way to do it. He simply has to trust
his own judgment and decide what is the most concise "code" for
a given situation, since clearly "the situation" is much larger than
"the code." However, being in the business of encoding, he ought
to behave as an encoder. He should make certain that the code he
selects is the best he can come up with. Hence, his contact with the
language should be maintained on a very technical level. He should
be aware of the existing usage; he should be aware of the language
which had died. In other words, he should "feel" the language
around him. He may feel an urge to use a word simply because it's
pleasing, but at the same time the social connotations of this particular word might have changed. Conversely, he might like to use

the word which had just emerged as a fad, not realizing that as a fad it may die very soon.

KLINKOWITZ: I was just going to ask you if you think, ideally, you can be sure that the reader will *have* the response that you calculate. How far do you think a writer can control his reader's response?

KOSINSKI: Clearly he cannot gauge the response of the readers; a novelist will never know what the response to his work is. He can poll all his friends and what he might receive might not be typical at all. The only way is to assume that the code he provides will trigger *some* response.

Hence, I believe, the more pertinent the code, the more of a response it will produce. One piercing can be felt more than fifteen taps on the shoulder. If you pierce someone with a small needle the response might be greater than, let's say, twenty-five moderate blows. The man can dismiss them: "Well, he hit me *several* times." That's all. For me to evoke more means to describe as little as possible. Trust the power of words. Trust the collective imagination. A writer does not create the reader's imagination; he merely evokes it. That's why a novelist must assume that if he writes it is not because his perception is different from others, but that his perception is similar to the perception of others and that the only difference between him and others is that he decided to sit down and to encode in language what others encode in metal, in clay, in concrete, and so forth.

If the purpose of fiction is to tap, so to speak, the imagination of the reader, then the novelist should always consider—indeed, like Western Union—the price of the words. I tend to believe that "the more" of the language, the less evocative its power. The danger begins when a novelist calls attention not to the entity he attempts to create through the language, but to the language, to the code itself. Language is also reality; words have specific independent existence. But if the language on the page attracts attention to itself, to the form, the way an actor once in a while attracts attention to himself rather than to himself as an actor, then the language fails as a conveyor. In the essay on *The Painted Bird* I speak of an actor as Hamlet. In the play, are we supposed to meet an actor, or are we supposed to meet Hamlet? We expect to meet Hamlet—not the actor.

KLINKOWITZ: How do you avoid that danger?

KOSINSKI: I discipline myself to write with a very clear notion of an incident I want to describe. First, I pick up words rather indiscriminately and I type them on the page almost as if it were a poem. And then I begin to remove as many of them as possible. This is the initial stage. I realize that during this process of de-escalating I am quite likely altering not only the language but to a degree the vision. There is a price I pay; perhaps language which I thus employ strips the incident of certain aspects, but, on the other hand, perhaps other aspects are made more perceivable. I feel that for a native novelist who is doing the same thing this process is very often unconscious. His promptings are the forces of his life, of his growing up, of his adolescence. I can't help remaining aware of every stage of my writing even though often I would like to forget. But I can't.

You asked me before about the relationship between the sociological awareness, and, let's say, the literary one; and I said that political writing is for me a sort of literature which aims at different properties—instead of projecting toward an individual situation, sociological imagination, for instance, aims at abstracting situations, larger social forces— which does not aim at a "finished form." My attraction towards sociology and political science was caused by their attempt at abstracting the totality of human experience.

The fact that some of the political writers would later become personally engaged in politics was to me an act of ultimate betrayal on their part as writers. A writer called Lenin later became a bureaucrat; a writer Mao turned into a bureaucrat; a writer (and art critic) Trotsky turned commissar of war. In terms of their creative ability, I found this tragic, since their language and their encoding had enormous appeal to a great number of people. Hence it once was literature. We might question its moral message (many critics question the morality of the protagonist of *Steps* or the morality of the Boy in *The Painted Bird*). However, one cannot deny that their encoding was properly chosen—Lenin, Trotsky, Mao did communicate with the masses of people they did not know; they did evoke certain emotional states, even purgatory ones, the reactions they could not foresee and predict.

The attempt to dismiss all of this sort of writing as a mere propaganda is, I think, something which future generations, if they will be here, would have to ponder. I think Hitler—in terms of the popularity of *Mein Kampf*—must be paid attention no less than popular novelists of the time. And Lenin and Stalin and Trotsky and Mao in terms of my life would certainly deserve attention as great fiction writers of the twentieth century.

KLINKOWITZ: How exactly do you see them as literary artists?

KOSINSKI: I see them as men who at the outset of their creative effort instead of opening a factory or starting a shop would use language, inking, a symbol, through which they attempted to abstract the major forces operating in a society, the major instincts, the minor vices—they wanted to evoke certain images, passions in their readers, and they achieved this; from a purely novelistic point of view, therefore, they aroused emotions. Some of their writing first purged men of their dangerous emotions, since anyone who read Lenin authentically hated the imaginary enemies of the proletariat, and in an Aristotelian fashion, during the act of reading, he was purged of dangerous emotion. The tragedy was that the writer who first managed to purge the emotions would feel that he had to purge people rather than their emotions.

I think the misfortune of Western culture is that often it calls on the writer to prove that he can physically do what he had imagined so well. And this temptation leaves none of us free. We all give in to it one way or another. I mean my talking to you right now is in a way my mistrust of my art and my believing that perhaps my fiction does need explanation. I think that this trend of Western culture makes us move towards a lower level of perception, towards the visual. The preoccupation with the image conveniently frees us from the predicament of being involved with the reality; now we can simply observe it.

KLINKOWITZ: I wonder; do you agree then that when the writer takes life and transforms it (by controlled selection) into what we call art there's this great danger that it might turn into life again and become truly potent?

KOSINSKI: Why is it a danger? I see the writer primarily as evoker. He merely taps what's there. He doesn't create any new worlds. He doesn't exist outside of the existent. He is not creator of new reality. He is merely a refocuser; not a transformer.

KLINKOWITZ: I like the metaphor, as you mentioned, of "tapping," because it seems that he taps the source of power and makes it available.

KOSINSKI: The power is there, yes. A human being is loaded with the greatest power—his imagination, the ability to transcend his own condition. No other creature, as far as we know, has the ability to transcend itself, to bypass the "real" condition. A dog cannot imagine itself as anything but a dog. Hence he cannot modify his existence in any way. He's at the mercy of the ultimate gravity—reality. But nothing prevents us from lifting ourselves above it. The greatest ability we have is the ability to transcend our own condition. The crudest man, the most crippled mind, the most retarded child, has an ability which no atomic bomb, no hydrogen weapon, could possibly create.

KLINKOWITZ: I was wondering if you feel art or fiction can be more real than reality. I'll read you a sentence from your *Notes of the Author*: "*The Painted Bird*, then, could be the author's vision of himself as a child; a *vision*, not an examination, or a revisitation of childhood."

KOSINSKI: Yes, such a vision is total. It encompasses any aspect of our temporality, of our empirical presence. Hence, our tangible confinement in time and space is inferior to the play of our imagination. In the moment of this interview you can see yourself conducting the interview with me, but nothing prevents you from "departing" (while you are still bodily here) to another presence.

In other words, the vision is always greater and truer, since a vision encompasses both the actual, "horizontal" condition and the transcendence into a new "vertical" mode, self-generating within its own confinement.

KLINKOWITZ: And art becomes the unique vehicle.

KOSINSKI: Art becomes the only vehicle which directly leads to this unique awareness and to this singularly human ability. What's more, art exists only because of it.

KLINKOWITZ: In *Notes of the Author* you talk about the function of memory as an artistic device. How memory *edits* is the word you use. I might say memory selects, memory filters.

KOSINSKI: I think memory discloses, since selecting, editing, and filtering would mean a conscious effort, or at least a consciousness of the fact of selecting; I think that memory discloses involuntarily in the process which we have no control of. We tend to perceive ourselves either in a very general way or in a minutely idiosyncratic one. And what fiction can do and what fiction has done, I think, was to bring certain functional elements into the awareness of our "reality." I don't think there's a possibility of truly knowing "the edges"; the reality fuses with our vision of it. The edges are like photographs developed on an aged paper—they are blurred, not clear.

KLINKOWITZ: Are remembered events fictions?

KOSINSKI: Yes, they are fictions; even though they accommodate "autobiographic elements" they are edited out. I think our notion of ourselves is a fiction which is composed of what we have memorized, edited, created, imagined. Our recollection contains, for instance, fleeting moments of the childhood, highly telescoped, a few events from the boyhood and adolescence. What else is there? There's no continuity. Is there a plot? A plot, a sense of destiny, is provided for us by family tradition, by society, by a political party, or by our own indoctrinated imagination. The plot is given by outsiders—parents, for example—who insist on destiny of some sort. Psychoanalysts would insist on a destiny we can't quite control;

Marxism insists on a societal destiny, on realized necessity; an existentialist points out our constant split and our tragic plight. What is our individual consciousness, or our individual awareness? It is composed of very short incidents. Our memory is the great short story writer. Maybe that is why we believe that everyone has one novel in him: his own empirical existence—if he can extract his self from it. I think it's quite appropriate: our memory is our supreme writer and editor. It is the aesthetic dimension of our life.

KLINKOWITZ: So these fictions are an accommodation to the past, then? Or they can be?

KOSINSKI: Your memory accommodates according to "the general style" of your mental fiction-writing process. In terms of your memory you, as a fiction writer, encode events of your life either by rejecting this "novel" of your life, or you encode them as highly acceptable and pleasing. In both instances you free yourself from the oppressive presence of everyday existence by substituting your own little fictions. The idea of the happy end, the notion of the tragic end, are all devices originated in our memory. By observing our memory we have arrived at a notion of writing fiction. Writing fiction is, after all, a recent enterprise; claiming that there is a clear pattern to individual life was reinforced when so many of the nineteenth-century philosophers supported the notion of destiny. We were surrounded by things which we were told had beginning and end and a purpose; we were surrounded by animals which would always behave in the same way; we were surrounded by social institutions which would start wars and make peace, but somehow our own life seemed to be composed of tiny little events selected at random. Why we would remember our father more than our mother, why we would remember a minor quarrel more than a serious one, why we would not recall a fight in which we had lost our teeth—all this bothered us, and the collective psyche came up with the notion of individual destiny. I think Freud—a great novelist of his time—supplied the notion that there is a plot to our life. Proust named the plot: remembrance of things past.

KLINKOWITZ: So you can't really control this part.

KOSINSKI: No, these are the blurred edges. These are the margins which we have not been able to manipulate at all.

KLINKOWITZ: You have described *The Painted Bird* as being the result of a slow unfreezing of a mind; are these the edges coming into focus?

KOSINSKI: Maybe not the edges, but only the central darkness. We often are polarized between the edges only, losing the sight of this central darkness. We give plot to our lives—pleasure, vice, fetish, family—"I am a businessman," "I am an engineer," "I enjoy my work," "I love my work," this sort of bland vision—without ever coming to terms with the essence of one's existence. The edges are easily lit, but the area between very often remains completely obscured. I think the unfreezing of the mind only fiction can accomplish . . . but it's only an unfreezing, it's all there.

There seems to be hidden in both the Protestant ethos and the Judaic ethos an excessive fear of this central darkness; the fear of the discovery of the real, not merely acceptable, reasons for our harassed existence; a certain mistrust of creativity, of imagination, as a force which illuminates the meaning of our lives.

This fear of imagination as a probing force is probably the reason why a work of fiction is so often ascribed to a specific experience of someone else who has experienced it and written about it and "it is autobiographical"; that is, the reader is excused from assuming that it might happen to him.

If literature has been a conveyor in this country, it was often a conveyor "moving backwards" to an act which had already taken place in the work of fiction—back to the author. This manifested itself often in those American writers who volunteered an imaginary act of ontological reduction in their novels, who would then attempt to prove that even though they hadn't done it before they wrote about it, they, as creators, had "to return" to the world of "lived experience," of empirical temporality. What a tragic reversal: imagination needing a stamp of approval from reality. I think such an attitude reflects fear of a work of fiction which abandons the personal self to address itself to a different reality which lies beyond the novelist's volition, and in which the reader might discover ("hear in retrospect") what without the novel he would have never suspected in himself.

KLINKOWITZ: Can we discuss more specifically the literary form of your works? All three of your fictional works are written in different forms. I wonder if you have any general idea about literary form that perhaps unifies this development.

KOSINSKI: I think the form of each novel stems very directly from what I wanted to say. I think the form reflects the specific content, and I couldn't think of any other form which would do it better.

For instance, everything I think about language was reflected in *Steps* by ascribing to the dialogue an independent function; *dialogue became an independent incident.* Each of the incidents in *Steps* is independent; they are connected by the picaresque, but they are also connected by the cumulative awareness of the protagonist— his awareness of the self and of the society. The destiny-oriented Western culture insists—even in a novel—on a guiding principle, and hence on a plot. Maybe that is why so many people found *Steps* extremely difficult to follow—some critics saw in *Steps* several different male protagonists—as if afraid to recognize that our lives are not based on a single plot; nor, for that matter, is our fiction.

Confronting oneself developed in *The Painted Bird* through the series of exposures with the natural world, with the supernatural world, with the societal world of the Boy. And in *Being There* the language avoids highly complex metaphors; it reverts primarily to a garden and to television, and that's all. In *Being There* the same double metaphorical system is operating for those who are not "on Chance's side": Benjamin Rand, his wife Elizabeth Eve, and people around them.

KLINKOWITZ: In our own day, in our own culture, do you think such a popular medium as television does anything to our concepts of time and space which in turn might be reflected in a literary work written from our times?

KOSINSKI: I think its impact is already visible. I think the American novelist will have great difficulty in fencing off the influence of television and of film, the media which have very short attention spans, which bombard quickly, which are gimmicky in their attitudes; but, conversely, some novelists will quite consciously try to do the very opposite.

Love Story, for instance, comes very close to a screenplay—it reads very much like a screenplay. Some of the novels of Jacqueline Susann, of Harold Robbins, of Wallace have that obvious cinematic dimension. And they were immediately translated into the medium which they resemble anyhow—into cinema. But on the other hand there may emerge a novelist who might not necessarily follow the easily perceivable pattern of TV and film.

KLINKOWITZ: I would also like to talk about the ideas in your books. John W. Aldridge has called you a philosophical novelist, a man concerned with the nature and meaning of the human condition.[2] Along this line I see in all five of your books, including the two on collective behavior, a basic concern with the individual in relation to other selves and to groups.

KOSINSKI: I guess I'm preoccupied in my nonfiction and in my novels with—what interests me most—the relationship between the individual and the group. During the war, as a child I lived in small villages, and as an unwelcome outsider I couldn't help noticing how each peasant personified the whole village, with all its system of beliefs, with all its systems of property. Perhaps then I realized that each of us is a microcosm of societal forces which operate outside and inside of us. I became aware of it again during the Stalinization of Poland, when for various political and ethnic reasons I was cast aside. By then, to a degree, I probably provoked some of it; I really didn't mind it. When I look at the pattern of my life I note that I often invite the penetrating force of society

2. *Saturday Review*, April 24, 1971, p. 25; also in *The Devil in the Fire: Retrospective Essays on American Literature and Culture, 1951–1971* (New York: Harper's Magazine Press, 1972), pp. 267–77.

to approach me—and to reproach me—for not giving in, to remind me, as it were, where I stand as an individual. I considered ideology to be basically a form of fiction.

I once remarked, and this almost removed me from the Soviet University for the third time, that in my view Stalin was "an ideal novelist," a kind of writer every writer secretly would like to be—to have your books published in millions of copies by the state (all the volumes beautifully bound) and to have all your potential critics arrested and exiled on the day of publication. What a dream! (By the way, no one in the history of literature could ever match Stalin, since he would not only arrest the critics who actually were critical of his work but even those who were potentially critical.)

I saw myself imprisoned in a large "house of political fiction," persecuted by a mad best-selling novelist, Stalin, and a band of his vicious editors from the Kremlin, and quite logically I saw myself as a protagonist of his fiction. What kind of a protagonist? I could have selected many examples from the Soviet literature which would somehow make me the cheerful inhabitant of a labor camp or a prison. But in my darkroom I also read *The House of the Dead*, and I really saw myself living inside of a "novel" called "the Soviet Union" created by the crude imagination of bad artists, and then I realized that my ultimate goal was to escape (if necessary, to die by committing suicide).

KLINKOWITZ: I would like to ask you about possible affinities which might exist between your work and the films of Roman Polanski. Did you know him in Poland? He was in Lodz. . . .

KOSINSKI: Yes. We have known each other since 1950. I was taking the history of film in the Lodz State Film School, where Polanski studied, since the University of Lodz, where I was studying, did not offer the history and theory of film, and as this was one of my minor subjects I was allowed to take the history and theory of film for two years at the Lodz Film School.

KLINKOWITZ: For two native Americans, if they had both come from, let's say, San Francisco at the same time, you would study these people for affinities that they might have. Do you think the same affinities spring from Lodz? Was there an essential experience?

KOSINSKI: I think there was an experience far more important than Lodz; it is commonly referred to as the Second World War. It is a film made with a lot of extras, some of whom were not destined to live through the film. We were both six years old when the war began, and our perceptions were quite likely similar. Then during the Stalinist period its totalitarian measures equally hit our idiosyncracies which we had developed to survive the war.

KLINKOWITZ: We've mentioned before how a liberated self can be a very terrifying thing, particularly because of the conditions which society sets up, which one has to work against to become liberated. Just last week I saw for the first time Polanski's movie from 1965, *Repulsion* (which is the same year that *The Painted Bird* was published) in which he presents the young girl in her apartment, excluded from society, totally within herself. Do you see tonal similarities between this film and *The Painted Bird*? The horror of the liberated self impressed me in both works.

KOSINSKI: A point well worth making. Perhaps war does accentuate both the "liberated" individual and the enforced collectivity. In 1939 in Central Europe a Jew who had considered himself a peaceful member of a community in which he was accepted became the ultimate threat to the safety of this community on the day of Nazi invasion. These rapid upheavals in the relationship between the individual and society were very clear already at the age of six to Polanski and to me. Suddenly, each of us became the enemy of our environment, and the environment turned into our supreme enemy. Maybe this accounts for some of our vision.

KLINKOWITZ: In *The Painted Bird*, the Boy, of course, does survive, he does maintain a self of sorts, but it seems a very terrible survival. I think in a battle between the self and society most people would probably favor the self and condemn the society as a terrible, repressive power. But I'm wondering if you would agree that maybe the self can have a terror all its own in its survival. I'm thinking of the Boy in *The Painted Bird*—all these images of death, power, control, and revenge; they become almost lyrical, as when the narrator recounts the bombing of the apartment building, with the walls tumbling down, the grand pianos spilling out, and so forth. . . .

KOSINSKI: Yes, the props of traditional individuality are being suddenly shattered.

KLINKOWITZ: Those are lovely lyrical images, one of the most beautiful passages in the book, and yet it is all death and destruction. There's also the scene where the peasant carpenter is tossed into the cistern, which is literally boiling with rats . . . that's a lovely lyrical image—how he is so almost beautifully devoured alive.

KOSINSKI: In our society destruction and death often have the embellishments of a beautiful ritual. Those who go to war march very lyrically. Wives are kissing husbands goodbye, and there are flags and music and usually blue sky. The war is ugly only for those who lost—for the pianos blown into pieces that cannot produce a tone anymore. Maybe this is the merciful part of our existence: when we die our destruction is given an acceptable form by those who survive us. The terrors of the self, once they are realized, are greater than the terrors of society because they lack the embellishments.

KLINKOWITZ: How?

KOSINSKI: Society penetrates the individual claiming that he cannot survive the terrors of the self without the protective blanket of societal rituals and institutions. Our religions, our myths, our taboos, our mores, all reflect it.

KLINKOWITZ: One last question: After fourteen years, do you imagine that you will remain in America?

KOSINSKI: I don't know.

KLINKOWITZ: You don't know?

KOSINSKI: I don't know. I don't want to live in a non-English-speaking country. I would like to retain direct access to the language.

KLINKOWITZ: Are there any particular reasons why you would

like to remain within the English language, since you know at least four or five, as I'm told?

KOSINSKI: I don't know them well. I couldn't possibly write in any of them. That's the reason. It's a simple but main reason. I can only write in English.

KLINKOWITZ: Oh, I see.

KOSINSKI: And I love English. I really do. I find it fitting my de-escalating process; it allows constant pruning more than French, more than the Slavic languages I know. Its verb is powerful: the language lends itself to the vision I have chosen for my art.

John Gardner

INTERVIEWED BY JOE DAVID BELLAMY AND PAT ENSWORTH

This interview is an amalgamation of conversations held with John Gardner by Pat Ensworth in the spring of 1973 at Northwestern University and by Joe David Bellamy at the University of Rochester on July 10 and 11, 1973.

PAT ENSWORTH: My association with John Gardner began when he was imported to teach a writing seminar at Northwestern University. A writing class is a unique way to become acquainted with someone; one's critical tastes and philosophical biases become evident more quickly than they might through ordinary social or professional contact. One fact became immediately clear: in a class where the typical undergraduate literary consciousness resounded with echoes of contemporary writers like Barth, Barthelme, Hawkes, and Pynchon, Gardner's perspective stood out in occasionally violent contrast. While many students tried to give their prose apocalyptical overtones and experimental flourishes, their teacher often reserved his praise for the most traditional (but "affirmative") boy-meets-girl stories. Gardner's references in the college newspaper to certain contemporary authors as "cynical bastards" may have been caused more by impatience with amateur journalism than by critical condemnation. But when this was followed by a

plea to the students to strive for "nobility" in their writing, I felt
that his unusual sensitivity definitely needed further exploration.

John Gardner has published five novels—*The Resurrection, The
Wreckage of Agathon, Grendel, The Sunlight Dialogues,* and *Nickel Mountain*—as well as a collection of tales, *The King's Indian,* and
an epic poem, *Jason and Medeia.* He is forty years old, regularly
teaches English at Southern Illinois University, lives on a farm, has
gray hair, and smokes a churchwarden. His novels employ more-
or-less traditional structures in their attention to the development
of plot and character; as an epic poem, *Jason and Medeia* returns
to an even earlier technique. Classical and medieval concepts
abound in both the subject and the style of his work. In an era of
explosive experimentation with the art of fiction, questions about
this author's perspective are inevitable.

JOE DAVID BELLAMY: Hearing that John Gardner would be in
upstate New York teaching at the University of Rochester Writers
Workshop, I drove down on a sunny, hot afternoon and met
Gardner and his wife, Joan, after a reading (by Judith Rascoe)
that night. Gardner is a well-built man of medium height with
light collar-length hair and very light eyes. He was wearing scuffed
boots, a red sports coat, and a pink tie. We had a late dinner at a
restaurant called Tale O' the Whale, where we were mistaken for
a bunch of hippies and got the poorest service imaginable; then we
came back to the Towne House Motor Inn, the place we both were
staying, a gaudy monstrosity in the S&H Green Stamp tradition.
In the room we pulled up a walnut-formica table, improvised
some coffee and tea makings in a scaly aluminum pot—while Joan
listened from the bed—and talked into my Sony TC120 until about
two in the morning.

BELLAMY: What fictional modes, would you say, are dead, and
which ones are still fertile and worth pursuing?

JOHN GARDNER: Before the Beatles, music was one way, and after
the Beatles, music has been another way. As a matter of fact, in
all the arts, the Beatles are a sort of turning point. With the squares,

however much one admires squares—I mean Hemingway, Faulkner, all those guys—the voice is always straight. You know they're
telling you this serious thing. Certainly they all have their ironies.
But basically Hemingway is going to tell you something true. After
the Beatles, it turns out everybody is writing an Elijah Thrush. You
can't tell where Purdy is in that because he is so much involved
in taking on a voice. Another way of saying this is: the tradition of
the short story and the novel as it came to be defined straight across
the forties and fifties gives way in the sixties to a sort of tale-
and-yarn tradition, where there is a distinct voice, a narrator, a guy
talking who is *definitely* not the writer and who is fun to listen to
and fun to watch and who tells you all kinds of things that may be
true and may be false.

BELLAMY: An unreliable narrator.

GARDNER: Right. Sure.

BELLAMY: Putting you on sometimes.

GARDNER: Right. . . . Robert Louis Stevenson, in an essay, talks
about the extremes in art. He sets up Victor Hugo at one extreme
and Fielding at the other. Victor Hugo is a guy who gives you
the streets of Paris, and you really feel you're there. Fielding, on
the other hand, gives you Tom Jones, and every time you start to
think Tom Jones is a real boy he throws something at you—like
a comic or Homeric simile or a battle in a graveyard or some crazy
thing—and you know this isn't real. . . . Up into the forties and
fifties we were all doing Hugo. In the middle sixties and now everybody is doing Fielding, suddenly tired of the small-minded seriousness of those novels, their delicate apprehensions, and going instead
for big emotions, going for big commitments, or for big jokes.
The Sot-Weed Factor is, I think, nothing but a big joke. It's a
philosophical joke; it might even be argued that it's a philosophical
advance. But it ain't like Victor Hugo. You're always aware of a
page.

BELLAMY: Why did this change come about? Is the idea that
writers should imitate nature a bad aesthetic idea?

GARDNER: Certainly nobody could say that the imitation of

reality is a bad idea. It is true, however, that if you keep imitating a particular aspect of reality over and over, stories start sounding an awful lot alike. Guys like Hemingway and Faulkner can make it because they're so great, but with all those third-rate writers it gets to be a bore. So, writers start finding other ways of getting to the same things, or to better things, or to different things. You're going for the dream-reality, for constructing universes, made-up worlds. But one of the things that makes any novel fun is that there's a world that's really real. It's a convincing dream. If you keep doing the realistic, John O'Hara world, the *Butterfield 8* world, it gets so it's the same world over and over. But when you write something . . . like the novel George Elliott is working on now. . . . A central character is an emperor of ancient Byzantium. You know, what a terrific idea! You can suddenly do all those settings and backdrops, and you can do girls in the way girls have never been done—because, you know, who knows what the girls in Byzantium were like? You can do . . . toys, you know . . . golden birds on a golden bough.

ENSWORTH: You've taught medieval literature for seventeen years. How has this influenced your writing?

GARDNER: I think I use the stylistic tricks of Chaucer more than those of any living man.

ENSWORTH: In what way?

GARDNER: For one thing, in the narrative voice. Often my narrator is a real made-up character who gets involved with the story. Chaucer does this in *Troilus and Criseyde*: the narrator describes a situation and then becomes carried away defending his characters. In the "Nun's Priest's Tale" when Chanticleer does something stupid (because he's only a chicken) the Nun's Priest gives every reason in the world why it isn't as stupid as it looks. In *The Sunlight Dialogues* when the narrator tells about Will Hodge, Sr., he throws out long, parody-Faulkner sentences in parentheses: "Invincible Hodge!" "Ah, Hodge!" He is carried away by his character. I'm not allowed to use these medieval techniques in *Grendel* and *The Wreckage of Agathon* because of the first-person narration, but they are present in *The Sunlight Dialogues* and in *The Resurrection*. I use lots of tricks Chaucer uses.

BELLAMY: Do you see any other connections between medieval literature and contemporary literature in terms of common modes that you find especially exciting?

GARDNER: Maybe it's just my imagination, but it seems to me we are a play out of the seventeenth century. Seventeenth-century civilization is us. The Middle Ages was the end of a different civilization. Someplace in the sixteenth century the Middle Ages stopped. In the fifteenth and sixteenth centuries all the genres break down. It becomes impossible to write a straight romance, or a straight anything. And everybody who is anybody starts form-jumping. Chaucer, for instance, starts putting together the epic poem. That's *Troilus and Criseyde*—it's a whole crazy different kind of thing. Well, and Malory comes out with *Morte d'Arthur*, which is a freaky new kind of form, a breakdown of all kinds of other forms. The mystery play arises. The literary genres of the Middle Ages didn't work anymore because the metaphysic and social ethic that supported them was no longer believed.

BELLAMY: Does your sense of the connection between your medieval work and your fiction encompass any special ideas about myth? Myth seems to interest a number of writers now, and *Grendel*, for instance, certainly seems to have those kinds of dimensions. Do you see that as a fertile direction that you plan to keep exploring?

GARDNER: It's very tempting to say, "Yes, I am working with myth because myth is so resonant"—it sounds good. . . . In *Grendel* I wanted to go through the main ideas of Western civilization— which seemed to me to be about . . . twelve?—and go through them in the voice of the monster, with the story already taken care of, with the various philosophical attitudes (though with Sartre in particular), and see what I could do, see if I could break out. That's what I meant to do.

BELLAMY: Do you go through all twelve major ideas in that book?

GARDNER: It's got twelve chapters. They're all hooked to astrological signs, for instance, and that gives you nice easy clues.

These are ideas which have been around from Homer's time to John Updike's time, and all good men have taken one side and all bad men have taken another side on these basic issues. *Because* they are ideas that go all through history, maybe the book resonates. For one thing, I keep echoing people, borrowing from people. I steal lots and lots of things all the time. If my stuff works at all, it's because there's one fusing vision. But I keep borrowing, so it does have a resonance that goes back into prehistory. I guess that's what myth does. That is, I am making up an organizing feature for a lot of stuff.

ENSWORTH: Do you have any American models for your writing?

GARDNER: Certain passages in Melville are models for me, particularly in *Pierre*—a serious approach which is nevertheless ironic, a peculiar detached tone which is nevertheless able to say real, affirmative things. William Gass reinforced some points of style I had learned independently; I don't know if he is a model, but he's someone of whom I am conscious. And then probably Walt Disney.

ENSWORTH: Walt Disney? I can see that in *Grendel*; monsters are certainly part of Disney's cast of characters.

GARDNER: Yes. In *Grendel* the subject matter is Anglo-Saxon, but the treatment is what Walt Disney would have done if he hadn't been caught up in the sentimentality of smiling Mickey Mouse.

ENSWORTH: What about *The Sunlight Dialogues*? That seems to be a more realistic book; the narrator is more omniscient, more encompassing than a cartoon figure can afford to be.

GARDNER: But if you look at the character of Clumly—hairless, with a great big nose and perfect teeth—he's a cartoon figure. Nobody ever looked like that. The three old Woodworth sisters are a cross between Poe and Henry James and Walt Disney. Think of the cop and robber going up to the door together, both funny little men, the cop carrying a box of flowers . . . there's an awful lot of cartoon in that. The magic tricks may be from real magicians I saw rather than from cartoons, but they're pretty cartoonish.

I remember when I was a kid and first saw *Snow White* I hid under the seat when the witch came on. I still hide under the seat when that witch appears; it's harder now because the seats have gotten smaller. And I think it's not just me. Everything Stanley Elkin has written from *A Bad Man* on, especially his latest unpublished work, is all cartoon. There isn't a realistic image in it . . . it's really Disney. Disney is one of the great men of America. He just had a weak streak, a poor silly sentimental streak. But America's got that too. Huck Finn's got it. Updike's got it. Some of us hide it better than others.

ENSWORTH: In *Grendel* and *The Sunlight Dialogues* you create characters who function as oracles: the Dragon and the Sunlight Man. Why did you choose this structure?

GARDNER: The Dragon looks like an oracle, but he doesn't lay down truth. He's just a nasty dragon. He tells the truth as it appears to a dragon—that nothing in the world is connected with anything. It's all meaningless and stupid, and since nothing is connected with anything the highest value in life is to seek out gold and sit on it. Since nothing is emotionally or physically connected you make piles of things. That is the materialistic point of view. Many people spend their lives, rightly or wrongly, doing nothing but filling out their bank accounts. My view is that this is a dragonish way to behave, and it ain't the truth. The Shaper tells the truth, although he lies. I don't know that there are any actual oracles in *Grendel*. There are in *The Sunlight Dialogues, The Wreckage of Agathon, Resurrection*, and *Jason and Medeia*.

And the real oracle in *The Sunlight Dialogues* is not the Sunlight Man. He's crazy; he's not an oracle at all. But there is an oracle; there's a real ancient sibyl in that novel. When Clumly is at a funeral one day (as usual, he's always going to funerals), an old Italian woman falls down and starts speaking Italian. She gives him oracular statements about the meaning of life and death.

Clumly doesn't understand Italian, and the little boy refuses to translate the final oracular statement, which has to do with *disanimata*—"disanimated." But Clumly comes to understand it at the end. He uses it in his mind during the last speech.

Yes, there are oracles in my novels. They are only partly metaphorical. Partly they are a metaphor for one who sees the totality, the connectedness, and is able to communicate it to other people, to make people see relationships. Partly it is a real mystical touch in me.

We have known for a long time that there are an enormous number of cases of apparent psychic response. For example, Baxter connected a polygraph to a gladiola on which a spider was living [see *Harper's*, November, 1972, p. 90]. He took away the spider, and the plant worried about its friend. Dogs have the ability to go thousands of miles to find the families they love. There are slightly less authenticated tests, like the alleged Russian experiment using a submarine and a family of rabbits. The mother rabbit was connected to an electrocardiograph; her baby rabbits were put on the submarine and killed. At every synchronized moment when one of her babies died, the mother rabbit's heart went kachoong. In other words, over a distance a radio can't reach, these impulses reached the mother without any time gap.

I don't believe or disbelieve things like this. I don't believe or disbelieve flying saucers or the alternate universe or antimatter or anything which can't be proved. Maybe they're true and maybe they're not, but it's good material for art. There are enough indications that these possibilities might be true that I don't mind affirming them, at least in a novel. In any case, they ought to be so.

BELLAMY: You indicate that the nihilistic dragon in the middle of *Grendel* is there to be repudiated; and now that you've brought this up, I see examples of other philosophies that you offer, in a sense, to repudiate. I wonder if you are able to state what philosophy, if any, you are advocating? In your essay, "The Way We Write Now," for instance, you say: ". . . it's in the careful scrutiny of cleanly apprehended characters, their conflicts and ultimate escape from immaturity, that the novel makes up its solid truths, finds courage to defend the good and attack the simpleminded."

GARDNER: That is hardly the description of a philosophical novelist, right? But I agree with that.

BELLAMY: In this essay you seemed very wrought up about moral values. I had the sense that you feel it is the writer's responsibility to perpetuate only what you see as "positive" moral values.

GARDNER: Yes, as long as those aren't oversimplified—like don't commit adultery, nonsense like that. . . .

BELLAMY: Right. But what would that be?

GARDNER: Generosity, hope, you know. . . . The ultimate moral value, the moral value I really look for beyond anything else, is to be exactly truthful—seeing things clearly, the *process* of art. Art is the absolute morality, because a good writer won't go to the next sentence until *this* sentence is perfect and says what's true. Then there are other kinds of things that value is related to—the sort of life-affirmation.

We're always at the mercy of critical fads. There was a period, a long period, when art was tied to moral statement. It was expected of any medieval artist, any Renaissance artist, that he would stand up for good principles—you know, support the queen. Then we got past that. It was clear that art doesn't really have to do that. You look at Chartres cathedral now, and it's just as beautiful as it ever was—you have the same holy feelings in it. But you don't know what all those little symbols are. What you know is about arches and light and expanses and rhythm. I think it still means the same thing as when it was built, but we don't talk about it in the same terms.

In more recent times, critics who had this sort of bias that art is supposed to be philosophy became uncomfortable with, say, Christianity—because it didn't seem to hold as a philosophy—or with nineteenth-century German idealism—because it didn't seem to hold as a philosophy. They began to love what are called "troubling visions." So I write a book in which there is a dragon who says everything a nihilist would say, everything the Marquis de Sade would say; and then at the end of the book there is a dragon who says all the opposite things. He says everything that William Blake would say. Blake says a wonderful thing: "I look upon the dark satanic mills; I shake my head; they vanish." That's it. That's right. You *redeem* the world by acts of imagination every time you pick up a baby. So that's a simple thing really.

You can't say *Grendel* is a peering into the abyss—nothing of the kind. It has none of that dignity. I am not Nietzsche, nor was I meant to be, nor would I want to be. I do *much* simpler things. I do the same thing guys who make sand castles do. I'm going to make damn good sand castles. That's really all. But, of course, at the same time, my sand castles make any little shanty that some guy builds on the beach look pretty silly.

Building sand castles is like the sculpture of Henry Moore. There's nothing profound about Henry Moore's sculpture. He does manage to find the rhythms of nature in stone or wood or bronze. He does manage to get the essence of a lady and her child—in bronze. In his old age he manages to build arches that look like pelvic bones in their flight against the sky in Florence. Magnificent things—but they're very simple. They don't refute Nietzsche or improve upon Kierkegaard. They're there, and you look at them, and you say: "Thank God for Henry Moore."

ENSWORTH: Why do you think the writer should be an affirmer of life?

GARDNER: I really do believe Shelley's idea about the poet as the legislator for mankind. My dream of the poet is a sort of African shaman, a poet-priest. Imagine a tribe has to go and hunt a tiger, and they're scared of the beast. A man stands up with his helpers and says a poem about how they're going to kill the tiger while his helpers play drums. By the time they've finished their one-day ritual, the poet makes them believe they can kill the tiger and the drummers make their hearts beat fast. The tribe goes out with their spears and that poor tiger's got trouble.

America has moved in the direction of the moving picture. You remember the days of *On the Waterfront*—the tipped-up collar, the cigarette hanging out of the mouth. A whole generation grew up tipping up their collars and hanging cigarettes out of their mouths. That's why we've got so much cancer in middle-age people now. Movies and comic books are the main popular art forms of our moment, and they do change the way people behave. As a writer, once you know this, or at least believe this, then you've got to ask, "Should I write *Straw Dogs* or should I write something else?" I think the answer is emphatically something else. Nobody's ever proved that television causes violence or that dirty movies cause dirty behavior. But if there's the vaguest suspicion, the least danger that it might be true, then a writer ought to think about it. I don't mean there should be no sex and no violence, and I certainly don't mean anyone should ban books. But a writer must decide how to treat these matters with a responsible concern.

People often say things they may or may not believe, like, "If I only had something that would make me get up in the morning." Most people do get up in the morning, but this kind of statement is popular. If writers reinforce it, pretty soon people are actually going to wonder why they do get up in the morning. And that's dumb. I'm most concerned with the trivial heroic acts of everyday life. These are the actions I want to remind readers of.

ENSWORTH: Shelley's view of the poet seems to be in conflict with the role you present in *Grendel*. The Shaper incites his community to war; Grendel sees him as a liar and a destructive force.

GARDNER: The Shaper comes along in a meaningless, stupid kingdom and makes up a rationale. He creates the heroism, the feeling of tribal unity. He makes the people brave. And sure, it's a lie, but it's also a vision.

Grendel is seduced by the Shaper: he wants to be a part of that vision. Unfortunately, he can't get in because he's a monster. But at the end of the novel Grendel himself becomes the Shaper. Beowulf bangs his head against the wall and says, *feel*. Grendel feels—his head hurts—so Beowulf makes him sing about walls. When the first Shaper dies, a kid is chosen to succeed him, but the real successor is Grendel. In the last pages of the book Grendel begins to apprehend the whole universe: life and death, his own death. Poetry is an accident, the novel says, but it's a great one. May it happen to all of us.

ENSWORTH: Then Grendel understands that the role of the Shaper —the role of the poet—is to apprehend, to feel, the whole universe?

GARDNER: Yes.

BELLAMY: Do you agree with Vonnegut then that the artist is the most important person in a society?

GARDNER: I guess all artists think that. I think all Xerox men think that the most important people are Xerox men. But I think that the most important are artists. They remind you of things that are obvious: human dignity, the terribleness of death, simple things.

BELLAMY: Is that your description of what a "philosophical novelist" should be doing too?

GARDNER: Stated in a slightly different way, this is my whole program. This is what I believe. I believe that the art of the thirties, forties, and fifties was fundamentally a mistake, that it made assumptions that were untrue about art, basically wrong assumptions that went wrong in the Middle Ages, too. They went wrong every time they were formulated as basic assumptions. And I think that their effect was to cut off readership.

When you think that art is a sophisticated way of thinking out problems and coming to understandings of things, then for one thing you start a story in the way that Jean Stafford starts a story— as if the story were happening inside the reader's consciousness. That kind of art makes you feel as if you ought to read stories because they're *good* for you; and, in fact, you can tell by the beginnings of those stories that those writers were assuming, "You will read this story because it's good for you." I don't think that has anything to do with it. That's not art; that part is just the sermon. The art is the arches and the light. What art ought to do is tell stories which are moment-by-moment wonderful, which are true to human experience, and which in no way explain human experience.

In the past there was a fundamental requirement that a writer was supposed to meet. Like, you read in the newspaper: "Henry shot Charlie." And you think: "*Why* did Henry shoot Charlie?" And the writer's program for a long time was to show you gradually how the moment came about that Henry shot Charlie. Then one day Kafka wrote: "As Gregor Samsa awoke one morning from a troubled dream, he found himself changed in his bed to some monstrous kind of vermin." You don't find out why he did that; you don't care why he did that. That's not the point. Barthelme writes: "An aristocrat was riding down the street in his carriage. He ran over my father." This is a sort of ringing affirmation of Kafka's rightness. In Bob Coover's story, "A Pedestrian Accident," a man is run over by a truck and thinks "Why me?" But then he thinks, "But that's a boring question," and the story goes on from there. We are not supposed to be doing psychology; psychology is not important. We are not supposed to be explaining motivation. Motivation is not important, and it never was important, for example, in those stories when some jinni would enter a person and do something. Motivation is the last thing from the Indian writer's mind in *Tales of Scheherazade*. That is, the motivation is always convincing—the characters always do what you think they're going to do—but it's not a study.

In American movies, for instance, you have this business of every time you have a mean lady in a movie, a lady who pretends to love a guy but she's willing to sacrifice his life for money, sooner or later there comes this boring part where she has to explain that she had a rough childhood—as if there were no other reason a lady would be a mean bitch. Sometimes people have wonderful happy childhoods and they still become mean bitches; but that's not the writer's business.

I don't think any of this is the writer's business. I think that we should not try to be sociologists, although it's fun to use sociology in a novel because a novel is a palace where you use anything that's decorative, anything that seems true. You don't have to be a psychologist, and you certainly don't have to be a painter of landscapes.

What you have to do, I think, is tell an interesting story. That means a plot that's kind of neat and that's got characters who are kind of neat and it happens in places that are made by the writer's imagination into "kind of neat." A plot that is kind of neat really is a plot that exercises the emotions of the reader and reminds him of his goodness or of his badness—you know, how *really* wicked he is. Any writer who pretends he's not a bad person, at least in some ways, is going to write pale stuff. To be Tolstoy you've got to be capable of writing the worst characters of Tolstoy with complete understanding as well as the best. That, I think, is what it is, and I don't think it's anything else. I think it has nothing to do with philosophy, although fiction uses philosophy as it uses everything else. And that's the break between contemporary writers whom I admire and earlier writers.

That's what I think fiction now is about. It's about creating circus shows. I *don't* think they're trivial. I think anybody who writes the way us guys write is going to be at the mercy of the critics—because we're going to be misunderstood.

BELLAMY: Who's "us guys"?

GARDNER: I think . . . guys who are storytellers—postsixties writers. I mean Stanley Elkin, Bill Gass, Donald Barthelme. . . . I don't know if they would be happy to be linked with me; so, you know, all apologies to them for my putting myself in their company. But I think they are fundamentally people making sideshows—but good, serious sideshows, because they raise you to your best, *not* philosophically, *not* morally.

BELLAMY: How does that jibe with your statement about the moral qualities that you would like to impart?

GARDNER: The moral qualities I want to keep are emotional qualities. The sense of courage that a reader shares vicariously with a character—when he goes out into the world he carries a little of that. . . . Remember your own personal emotion when you finished *Anna Karenina* the first time? You walk around for about two weeks in Russia, no matter what you're doing in Brooklyn or

wherever you are. You're living in Tolstoy's world, and you're living by Tolstoy's values—good art does that.

BELLAMY: Why all the philosophical meanderings then?

GARDNER: I think I'm a philosophical novelist, but that doesn't
mean a philosopher. That is to say, I'm a novelist, one of whose
main materials is the philosophical ideas of the twentieth century.

BELLAMY: But you don't see your purpose as working out the
right ideas in the end. Ultimately, you're not offering a system.

GARDNER: What I think is "right" is implicit in drama. So, I'm
not answering, say, Kant; I'm dramatizing Kant. My business is
drama. I can write a novel that doesn't have any philosophy in it
at all.

BELLAMY: A novel, then, according to your definition, would
become a kind of program for emotional experiences for the reader?
If the story is told well, and if the form is constructed with proper
elegance, and if the moral values are right, then the reader will have
this therapeutic experience—almost in the Aristotelian sense?

GARDNER: Sure. Absolutely. I would say it's very much in the
Aristotelian sense.

ENSWORTH: You stated in your July, 1972, article for the *New
York Times Book Review*, "The Way We Write Now," that "after
a period of cynicism, novelists are struggling . . . to see their way
clear to go heroic." How do you know the period of cynicism
is over?

GARDNER: With a few notable exceptions, the things people are
writing lately have changed tone completely. Joyce Carol Oates is
one writer who is now reassessing her whole career. She's thirty-
five, she's gotten the National Book Award, she's published novel
after novel, millions of stories—but it was always the same Joyce
Carol Oates. In her fiction the world seemed terrifying; she dealt
with this feeling by recording it and eliciting sympathy. Suddenly,
for mysterious reasons, she has flown up above that world and has
begun to look at it from very high up. She sees more beauty, more
compassion among characters, and she's turning quasi-mystical.
Joyce is a model of the writer who is finding a different attitude, a

more heroic and responsible approach. Stanley Elkin is another example: he used to write funny, cynical pieces, and now his work verges on a noble sort of sentimentality.

Most writers today are academicians: they have writing or teaching jobs with universities. In the last ten years the tone of university life and of intellectuals' responses to the world have changed. During the Cold War there was a great deal of fear and cynicism on account of the Bomb. Cynicism is a reaction to fear, a way of covering it. That atmosphere has gradually moved out in recent years. The Vietnam War is a terrible event, but it isn't a cause for cynicism. A very large, solid part of America which we thought was moneygrubbing and cynical was strongly against the war, and it becomes hard to maintain your cynicism when the people around you are all working hard to make the world better.

Notable exceptions to this are writers who very carefully stay out of the mainstream and therefore can't be influenced by the general feeling of people around them. For instance, Thomas Pynchon believes we're on our way to apocalypse. He jokes about this in *Gravity's Rainbow*. The whole novel becomes a huge, whinnying laugh about inevitable destruction. Pynchon stays out of universities. He doesn't know what chemists and physicists are doing; he knows only the pedantry of chemistry and physics. When good chemists and physicists talk about, say, the possibility of extraterrestrial life, they agree that for life to be evolved beyond our stage, creatures on other planets must have reached decisions we now face. That is, they must have seen their way past war, they must have dealt with their own hostilities and aggressions, and so on. These kinds of things were not said by scientists ten years ago when Pynchon was in close contact with them.

If a writer is around people (which is his business, because they're his subject matter) and if he lives in this age, then he has to see that all the worrying and whining we did in the last generation was futile and wrong-headed.

ENSWORTH: I don't understand the basis of your optimism. Certainly there have always been people working to improve the world, to do away with war. What makes this generation different from any other?

GARDNER: What happens in the modern world, in any period of progress, is not that some great man comes along with a grand solution. Not some great man, but a bunch of little people working on a bunch of little problems. Think of the issues we yelled about in the thirties, the crises which made intellectuals communists. None of these issues is still around; for example, everyone is unionized now, and it's no longer a problem. Every single one of these issues was solved not by a grand political overthrow, the kind of change intellectuals hoped for then. They were solved by gradual breakthroughs, little by little, by unknown people. I think we have to recognize that the age of great genius is over. We hoped John Kennedy was a great man, but during his administration we were becoming mired in the worst war we've ever fought. On the other hand, something much more stable is emerging: an informed public. Sometimes the informed public says stupid things, and sometimes it elects leaders who represent its worst interests, but when thing are stabilizing it becomes ridiculous to be a man crying wolf.

So, I think we're free to do what art ought to do, which is to celebrate and affirm. Obviously one can't turn one's back on dangers. We have to fight any tendency for the United States to become again the kind of monster it was for a while. After Vietnam we do have to worry about the evil which can come from isolationism and complacency. We must worry above all about righteousness, the kind of cheap righteousness which asserts that all crime is a terrible evil and all law-abidingness is a high virtue. One mentions these dangers in novels. Of course, a beautiful affirmation is meaningless if it doesn't recognize all the forces going against it.

ENSWORTH: How does the novelist "go heroic"?

GARDNER: He becomes an affirmer of life instead of a whiner against it. He takes responsibility and recognizes responsibility in other writers and in other people. He sees through complacency and righteousness. No hero is ever righteous: a hero makes mistakes, recognizes them, says, "I made a mistake," and tries to do something about it. He affirms the goodness of life and the badness of thinking you've got the whole answer.

ENSWORTH: Who are your heroes?

GARDNER: Homer is a hero, and so is Chaucer. Then there are some writers working right now to change their ways of writing, to enlarge their vision. John Updike is an example of this; John Cheever is another. A number of writers at this moment are doing a good job of reassessing themselves.

BELLAMY: In that same essay, "The Way We Write Now," you claim that current writers are "doomed by indifference to novelistic form." Many writers feel there is a great deal of consciousness of form right now—perhaps more than there has been for a long time. What do you mean by "novelistic form"? How can you possibly argue that current writers are indifferent to it?

GARDNER: You're right to ask: What do I mean by "novelistic form"? I think the novel is a different thing from a lyric, okay? I think that novelistic form is fundamentally plot form, development of a story, the Aristotelian *energia*, the actualization of the potential which exists in character and situation.

Grendel, for instance, is indifferent to novelistic form. I think that's okay—you can get away with it as long as you keep it short—but there are a number of problems in *Grendel*. At about Chapter 8 there is a section in which you are no longer advancing in terms of the momentum toward the end. It's just holding a slow movement, but it's a fake slow movement. We have now developed the whole position of Grendel, you know; it jells when Grendel meets the dragon. At this point, nothing more happens to Grendel. He's just waiting to meet Beowulf. Chapters 8, 9, 10—it's just the wheels spinning. That is *not* novelistic form; it's lyrical form.

BELLAMY: So, novelistic form is inexorable plot development working itself out—present action always progressing toward the outcome? Rising action, climax, and denouement?

GARDNER: Yes. When I say that people are doomed by an indifference to novelistic form, I'm thinking of some specific failures. Bill Gass and Stanley Elkin, for instance. I'll talk about them be-

cause they're my heroes. It seems to me that in *Omensetter's Luck*
you have this wonderful beginning, and this wonderful denouement, and then you have this middle, which is the Jethro Furber
section. It just goes on and on, self-congratulating and telling dirty
jokes and doing things that are not moving Furber anyplace. You
need that section, but you need about one-third of it, really. Of
course, Gass isn't interested in putting in the break and moving to
the next thing. He's just going.

Stanley Elkin has a different kind of problem, I think. He doesn't
have any glue in his stories. His stories are one stand-up joke after
another—wonderful, you know, brilliantly built lines and sentences
and situations, but no glue going from situation to situation. That
is to say, there is no novelistic theme which inevitably pushes you
through the plot. His plots are the ultimate in existential whimsy—
what new funny thing can I think of to say? And since he's so
funny, and since he's so special, I say, "Okay, Stanley, go ahead,"
and I keep reading. But it doesn't have the impact, doesn't have the
weight, the solidity, the force, that it would have if you feel yourself
slowly being bulldozed.

ENSWORTH: *Grendel* and *The Sunlight Dialogues* demonstrate
the struggle of mighty adversaries: Grendel and Beowulf and the
Sunlight Man and Clumly. Do you feel there are any mighty adversaries left in the world?

GARDNER: Faith and despair have always been the two mighty
adversaries. You don't have to see it in the way of a Christian,
Hindu, Buddhist, or any other system. A healthy life is a life of
faith; an unhealthy, sick, and dangerous life is a life of unfaith. If
you're going to drive from here to downtown Chicago you get in
your car and assume that the cars coming at you are going to pass,
not hit you head-on. They assume the same thing about you. That's
called faith. It doesn't work all the time; that's why faith can never
be codified. On the other hand, if you assume that everything's out
to get you, it's going to get you. You're going to be so worried which
direction it's coming from that you're not going to be looking in the
right direction. Faith is a physical condition, a feeling of security

which enables you to think about what you're doing and yet be subconsciously alert. Whereas unfaith, paranoia, is a total concentration which makes it impossible for your psyche and body to be alert. You concentrate on what's going to happen to you and there's nothing floating underneath. I don't know if that's medically sound, but I believe it.

ENSWORTH: Why is it that in both *Grendel* and *The Sunlight Dialogues* the characters with the most imagination are defeated or killed by men of lesser vision, mere functionaries like Beowulf or Clumly?

GARDNER: That question is not the center of *Grendel*, though it is of *The Sunlight Dialogues*. The Sunlight Man does have imagination; he imagines all the possibilities of the world. These possibilities are disparate and atomic, in the sense of particles not related to other particles. The Sunlight Man can see into all sorts of crazy alternatives, but he finds no order, no coherence in it. He's a wild, romantic poet with no hope of God. The two characters who have the most imagination in the novel are Clumly and Mrs. Clumly, because they can see into other people's minds. With his little mole's intelligence, Clumly stares at the Sunlight Man and tries to understand him. He really tries to understand the principle of evil by empathizing with it.

During the novel, the Sunlight Man, because of his experiences, sees fire around him. He knows that's crazy, but he keeps on seeing fire. Just before his last speech, Clumly looks through a door and sees it's burning inside: he's gotten inside the Sunlight Man's emotions. He fully understands even though he can't make sense of it. At least he has compassion, which is a kind of imagination.

At one point Clumly and Mrs. Clumly are lying in bed together. He thinks of her as a chicken—he wouldn't be surprised to see her feet sticking in the air. Later, Mrs. Clumly lies in the bed trying to sense what she looks like. It comes to her in a great flash: she looks like a chicken. Mrs. Clumly is the Beatrice of *The Sunlight Dialogues*. She guides everybody because she loves. This is the kind of imagination which holds the world together.

The ability to be patient, to be tolerant, to try to understand and empathize, is the highest kind of imagination. The ability to make up grand images and to thrill the reader is a nice talent, but if it doesn't include love, it's nothing—mere sounding brass.

ENSWORTH: What are your writing habits? When, where, and how do you write?

GARDNER: I write as much as I can. I get up early in the morning, stay up late at night, and write all the time. When I have nothing else to do, I write. Luckily, because of my university, sometimes I can go someplace far away where I'm protected from my own weaknesses. Not that I consider writing a duty—but since I have a family of whom I am very fond, and a teaching job with students of whom I am very fond, and we have friends who visit us, I often don't get much writing time in. When I go somewhere I don't know, it takes us two or three months to build up a circle of friends and thus interrupt my work.

I work from rhythms more than anything else—the way a sentence sounds in terms of rhythmical structure and the words you choose because of that structure. If a character isn't convincing, if a lady in a novel says something you think she wouldn't say, that's bad. If an action doesn't seem inevitable, that's bad. But the real heart is nevertheless the rhythm.

If I have any doubts about what a character would say or what a room would look like, I ask my wife. She has the ability to go into a room where she doesn't know anyone and tell you the first names of several people because they seem the Raymond type or the Sheila type. My writing involves these two imaginations in a very deep way, page after page after page. My own imagination is poetic and philosophical. I'm concerned with the rhythms of sentences and paragraphs and chapters, and with ideas as they are embodied in characters and actions. Joan's imagination is a very close psychological and sociological one. It informs everything I do. Perhaps I should have used "John and Joan Gardner" on the titles all along; I may do this in the future. But in modern times such a work is regarded as not really art. The notion that art is an individual and unique vision is a very unmedieval and unclassical view. In the Middle Ages it was very common to have several people work on one thing; the thirteenth-century Vulgate cycle of Arthurian romances had hundreds of writers. I feel comfortable with this approach, but I haven't felt comfortable telling people it's what I do. As I get more and more into the medieval mode, I'll probably admit how many writers I have.

BELLAMY: You leave it sounding as if your wife is a collaborator. Has she actually written parts of your books?

GARDNER: Frieda Lawrence did the same thing for D. H. Lawrence. It's not new. To have the attitude toward writing that I have at this moment is unfashionable, but I'm a medievalist, and in the Middle Ages they go in for the object, right? If you're making a cathedral, you don't worry about the abbot getting all the credit. You get the best mason you can, and so forth. I use a lot of people, Joan in particular. She hasn't actually written any lines, because Joan's too lazy for that. But she's willing to answer questions. The extent of her contribution doesn't quite approach collaboration in the modern sense.

BELLAMY: How do you manage to be so prolific? I see there are two more of your books scheduled for publication next year.

GARDNER: It's not because I'm prolific. For a long period of time, my writing was not liked. It was very difficult for me to get published; it was a very long period of time before I did. Finally people began to publish my things. Actually, *The Wreckage of Agathon* broke it, and I got a sort of mild reputation—although it's a kind of terrible book. Then after that *Grendel* got a sort of underground reputation, and then people were willing to risk *The Sunlight Dialogues*—although nobody had any confidence in it. In fact, I had sent it to every publisher there is. Nobody would touch it. One guy wrote the only encouraging thing, "We'll take it if you cut a third." I wrote back and said, "Which third?" I *have* written hard. I have worked on techniques hard. I have done exercises for years in sentences—working full days, paring sentences, learning to do things with sentences. People talk about my pyrotechnic stuff as if it was some little funny skill I have, but it's something, maybe the only thing, I've worked very hard for. Anyway, I wrote this stuff all the time. I've written lots and lots of novels. Some of them were conscious exercises to see if a certain thing could be done with form, because, I admit, I do love experiments in form. Anyway, I'm not fast. I work very hard and very long, and eventually I inch out a novel. But when you've been sitting writing for fifteen years, and nobody liking you, you do build up a backlog. I've been publishing an early work, a late work, an early work—it's kind of weird. *The Sunlight Dialogues* is an early work; *Grendel* is a late work; *Nickel Mountain*, coming out next year, is a very early work. Right after that comes my newest thing, *The King's Indian and Other Fireside Tales*, a very jazzy technical thing. That and *Jason and Medeia* are my two newest things.

BELLAMY: Could you actually set out again to write a book like *The Sunlight Dialogues*, which still seems more or less in the realistic tradition?

GARDNER: I don't see *The Sunlight Dialogues* as a book in the realistic tradition. I've always written kind of fabulous, weird stuff. In *The Sunlight Dialogues* I wanted to tell a story which had the feel of total fabulation, total mystery—magicians—strange things and impossible tricks—so that everybody would have the sudden feeling at some point in the novel that he's caught inside a novel, but with streets that can be recognized, houses which are accurately described, and so on. I wanted to tint the stock and photograph Batavia. I wanted to make people in the novel just as much like Batavians as possible and yet create the feeling that the whole novel is taking place in Oz. It may or may not have succeeded. I've talked to a lot of people who have been to Batavia since reading the novel, and the reaction was that it was a dull, drab, kind of colorless town, and yet everything I said was true. That is, the houses are exactly the color I said, everything is just as I said, but it's not like that at all. Okay, that's me again, playing tricks. As long as critics feel that novelists should be these terribly serious people, not at all like people who just make wonderful sand castles, then I'm gonna get killed. But I think wonderful sand castles are terrific; I think they're moral. I think they make you a better person much more than a sermon does. I like Barth's funhouse metaphor. I think it's right. Every writer now is lost in the funhouse—and pretty happy with it.

BELLAMY: I suppose this is a question that literary historians will worry about in fifty years, but do you think there is any sense of real coherence among those writers who emerged in the midsixties, who were lost in the funhouse and happy to be there, madly building sand castles and fantasizing to their hearts' content? Is there enough in common among them to start talking about these people as a group or as a "generation"?

GARDNER: Yes, there is. There really is, and I don't know what it is. At Northwestern I recently heard Jack Hawkes read from his new book, and I could hardly get my breath. I loved it; it's really fantastic. He does these things. . . . I mean, it's like a jazz musician listening to another jazz musician. There are a lot of differences between us, of course—literary historians will see great differences that we don't see clearly. There are very deep differences from a philosophical point of view between Bill Gass and me, for instance. But at least everybody's going for the same goal.

BELLAMY: Except Tom Wolfe.

GARDNER: Yep, right. Sure. Sure. There are a lot of good writers who don't have anything to do with the group we've been talking about.

BELLAMY: What do you think really happened in the midsixties when so many writers started changing? Is that an impossibly difficult question to answer?

GARDNER: Sunspots [laughing]. I don't know. I have no idea why things live as long as they do and then die. Maybe it happened earlier in music and art, and literature, being more complex, caught up late. But it happened in all of the arts, you know, within the second quarter of this century and petering into the third quarter.

BELLAMY: What happens next?

GARDNER: I think people are going to continue to be fairly conservative about form. People will continue to be hung up on formalism, consciousness of technique. There will, I think, be more Brautigans, and they will be an increasingly raucous element.

BELLAMY: What is a "Brautigan"?

GARDNER: Brautigan's concern is not with a well-built box. It's with a voice, an intuition, a hypothetical reaction, and making up things in a wingding fashion. . . .

BELLAMY: What else?

GARDNER: I think that where it's going for a while is where it is. This movement that you're talking about, and tracing, is solidly here and is the darling of the New York literary establishment—and for good reason. The real advances or changes are going to be totally dependent upon individual genius and freakiness. *Nobody* could have predicted Barthelme, you know. He wasn't a possibility. Then, suddenly, here he is!

Kurt Vonnegut, Jr.

INTERVIEWED BY JOHN CASEY AND JOE DAVID BELLAMY

He is a huge, slouching, loose-jointed man with a really impressive mustache. He talks easily, this great wounded bear of a man, and when he laughs, he booms. He has a presence, like a politician, without being portly. He fills a room. He is moody, truculent one instant, laughing contagiously the next. Kurt Vonnegut, Jr., is perhaps the best-known, if the least self-conscious, innovator among American contemporaries. Read by the millions, his novels *Player Piano*; *The Sirens of Titan; Mother Night*; *God Bless You, Mr. Rosewater*; *Cat's Cradle*; *Slaughterhouse-Five*; and *Breakfast of Champions*; plays *Happy Birthday, Wanda June* and *Between Time and Timbuktu*; and stories in *Welcome to the Monkey House* have made Vonnegut a cult figure and a cultural hero in his own time.

Parts of the following interview were conducted in the winter of 1968 during a visit by Vonnegut to the Iowa Writers Workshop, where he had taught from 1965 to 1967. For details of the visit, see *The Vonnegut Statement* by Jerome Klinkowitz and John Somer (Delacorte/Seymour Lawrence and Delta, 1973). The interview was expanded and updated in the summer of 1973 by additional questions, which were relayed to Vonnegut by telephone.

KURT VONNEGUT: I know you'll ask it.

JOE DAVID BELLAMY: Are you a black humorist . . . ?

VONNEGUT: You asked it. One day in solitude on Cape Cod, a large bell jar was lowered over me by Bruce Friedman, and it said "black humor" on the label; and I felt around a bit and there was no way I could get out of that jar—so here I am and you ask the question. At the time, I didn't know what "black humor" was, but now because the question must be asked, I have worked up what is called a "bookish" answer.

In the Modern Library edition of *The Works of Freud*, you'll find a section on humor in which he talks about middle-European "gallows humor," and it so happens that what Friedman calls "black humor" is very much like German-Austrian-Polish "gallows humor." In the face of plague and Napoleonic wars and such things, it's little people saying very wry, very funny things on the point of death. One of the examples Freud gives is a man about to be hanged, and the hangman says, "Do you have anything to say?" The condemned man replies, "Not at this time."

This country has made one tremendous contribution to "gallows humor," and it took place in Cook County Jail (you'll have to ask Nelson Algren who said it). A man was strapped into the electric chair, and he said to the witnesses, "This will certainly teach me a lesson."

Anyway, the label is useless except for the merchandisers. I don't think anybody is very happy about the category or depressed about being excluded from it—Vance Bourjaily was and took it very well, I thought.

JOHN CASEY: And the science-fiction label . . . ?

VONNEGUT: If you allow yourself to be called a science-fiction writer, people will think of you as some lower type, someone out of the "mainstream"—great word, isn't it? The people in science fiction enjoy it—they know each other, have conventions, and have a hell of a lot of fun. But they are thought to be inferior writers, and generally are, I think—at least the ones who go to conventions.

When I started to write, I was living in Schenectady, working as a public relations man, surrounded by scientists and machinery. So I wrote my first book, *Player Piano*, about Schenectady, and it was published. I was classified as a science-fiction writer because I'd included machinery, and all I'd done was write about Schenectady in 1948! So I allowed this to go on. I thought it was an honor to be printed anywhere. And so it was, I suppose. But I would run into people who would downgrade me. I ran into Jason Epstein, a terribly powerful cultural commissar, at a cocktail party. When we were introduced, he thought a minute, then said, "Science fiction," turned, and walked off. He just had to place me, that's all.

But I continued to include machinery in my books and, may I say in *confidence*, in my life. Most critics, products of humanities and social science departments, have felt fear of engineers. And there used to be this feeling amongst reviewers that anyone who knew how a refrigerator works can't be an artist too! Machinery is important. We must write about it.

But I don't care if you don't; I'm not urging you, am I? To hell with machinery.

CASEY: Are there science-fiction writers you admire?

VONNEGUT: Yes. Ray Bradbury, Ted Sturgeon, Isaac Asimov, among others.

CASEY: One of the sections of *Sirens of Titan* I'm very fond of is the chapter on harmoniums. But most of the book is so sardonic that I was surprised by the lyricism of the section. Did you mean this as relief? The way Shakespeare has comic relief?

VONNEGUT: I hope my relief is more helpful than Shakespearean comic relief.

CASEY: Did you intend . . . ?

VONNEGUT: Yes, I can say it probably was because at one point I used to talk about what I was going to do to lighten it up for a while. . . . Well, I don't think that way anymore. There was a time when I was a very earnest student writer and had a teacher, Kenneth Littauer, an old-time magazine editor, agent, and splendid old gentleman. And we would talk about things like that, that is, after dark passages you have a light one . . .

CASEY: . . . and there should be large and small shapes and in-between shapes . . .

VONNEGUT: . . . and use short sentences with short words when people are running, and long sentences and long words when people are sleeping. Those things are all true, the things I learned from Littauer about pace and point of view, things that are discussed in *Writer's Digest*, decent and honorable things to know. We must acknowledge that the reader is doing something quite difficult for him, and the reason you don't change point of view too often is so he won't get lost; and the reason you paragraph often is so that his eyes won't get tired, is so you get him without him knowing it by making his job easy for him. He has to restage your show in his head—costume and light it. His job is not easy.

CASEY: Is this still the way you write?

VONNEGUT: I don't know. I have this strong sense of merely un-folding. I let the old ghost use me when he feels he can.

BELLAMY: Could you talk a little bit about your method of composition, how you write and rewrite successive pages one at a time?

VONNEGUT: Yeah, well there are the swoopers and there are the bashers, and I happen to be one of the bashers. That is, you beat your head against a wall until you break through to page two and you break through to page three and so forth. A lot of people write just any which way. I have absolutely no use for an electric type-writer, for instance; I still can't imagine why the damned thing was invented. But the swooper's way, you know—and I envy them, too, because it must be exhilarating—is to write a book any which way in a month maybe, whack it out, and then go through it again and again and again and again. I've never been able to do that. I came close to doing it on *The Sirens. The Sirens* was a case of automatic writing, almost. That wasn't a bashing book because I just started and I wrote it.

CASEY: This girl I know says that Kurt Vonnegut dislikes women.

VONNEGUT: You know, I think I get along with women quite well. In my life, in my actual life, I hope I don't treat them disparagingly. It has never worried me but is puzzling that I've never been able to do a woman well in a book. Part of it is that I'm a performer when I write. I am taking off on different characters, and I frequently have a good British accent, and the characters I do well in my books are parts I can play easily. If it were dramatized, I would be able to do my best characters on stage, and I don't make a very good female impersonator.

And also there is the resentment I had against my wife. Everybody gets pissed off at his wife, and when I'd be angry at her and there's a houseful of kids and so forth—you know there *were* these shattered realities in my life—I'm working in a houseful of diapers and my wife wanting money and there not being enough and so forth. I was angry with my wife for the same reason everybody is angry with his wife. And I'm not anymore. The children are all grown up. Maybe I can write better about it now.

CASEY: Is Winston Niles Rumfoord in *Sirens of Titan* a verbal portrait of FDR? There are hints—the cigarette holder, high Groton tenor, and details like that. Was FDR part of the impulse to write the book?

VONNEGUT: You know, no one else has ever commented on that. The fact is Roosevelt is the key figure in the book, although the impulse was to write about what FDR had been to me as a young man during the Depression and the Second World War and so forth. Roosevelt took the lead in the book, however, not me. As I say, I wrote that book very quickly. I hadn't written a book for maybe eight years, and a friend of mine, Knox Burger, an editor, saw me one day and said, "Write me a book!" I had an idea; he liked it. I went home and very cheerfully and very quickly produced it. Almost automatic.

BELLAMY: Could you elaborate a bit on how FDR became a key figure in *The Sirens of Titan*?

VONNEGUT: Well, Franklin Roosevelt was one of the biggest figures in my childhood. He was elected to his first term when I was ten years old. And he spoke with this aristocratic Hudson Valley accent which nobody had ever heard before, and everybody was

charmed. You know, here was an American. And we do love it so
when we find a dignified American, like Sam Ervin is, speaking
with an accent. And this accent of Kennedy's is described as a Harvard accent. It isn't at all; it's an Irish, middle-class, Boston accent,
which was charming too. People loved to hear him talk; it was
English, you could understand it and all, and it was musical. So
having been born with an empty mind, an awful lot of it was filled
with Franklin Roosevelt who was president during sixteen years
of my life.

BELLAMY: Well, do you think there are any analogies between
what Rumfoord does in the novel and perhaps what Roosevelt did
socially and politically—as a major changing force in the country?

VONNEGUT: They both have enormous hope for changing things
. . . childish hopes, too. I don't think Roosevelt was an enormous
success except as a personality. And maybe that's the only kind of
success a president needs to have anyway.

CASEY: Are there any other people . . . ?

VONNEGUT: Well. Eliot Rosewater, for instance, in *God Bless
You, Mr. Rosewater*—there really is a man who is that *kind*. Except
he's poor, an accountant over a liquor store. We shared an office,
and I could hear him comforting people who had very little income,
calling everybody "dear" and giving love and understanding instead of money. And I heard him doing marriage counseling, and
I asked him about that, and he said that once people told you how
little money they'd made they felt they had to tell you everything.
I took this very sweet man and in a book gave him millions and
millions to play with.

BELLAMY: Another thing: it's a minor point, but people I've
talked to are troubled that in your works you use a lot of the same
characters but you . . . from novel to novel you make slight changes
in their names, such as Bernard B. and Bernard V. O'Hare, Helga
Noth as Howard Campbell's wife in *Mother Night* and then Resi
North in *Slaughterhouse-Five*. Is there any conscious intent behind
these changes?

VONNEGUT: Well, no, only a perversity to not look in a former book. I don't look in a former book. And it's just a perversity that comes from having written so long, I guess. Just fuck it, it doesn't really matter what their names are. You look at old copies of the *Writer's Digest*; there's article after article on how to pick names for characters.

CASEY: In *Cat's Cradle*, where did you get the idea for Ice-9?

VONNEGUT: Irving Langmuir, a Nobel Prize winner in chemistry, told H. G. Wells, as an idea for a science-fiction story, about a form of ice that was stable at room temperature. Wells wasn't interested. I heard the story and, as Langmuir and Wells were both dead, considered it my legacy, my found object.

At a cocktail party once I was introduced to a famous crystallographer, and I told him about Ice-9. He just dropped out of the party, went over to the side of the room, and sat down, while everybody was chatting away, for a long time; then he got up and came over to me and said, "Uh-unh, not possible."

CASEY: ... Childhood ... ?

VONNEGUT: Here are two things that ruined my earlier life: life insurance and envy.

When I became a writer, I quit General Electric, had a family, and moved to Cape Cod, which was an alarming thing to do. It frightened me so much about what might happen to my family that I bought a perfect bruiser of a life insurance policy. Every nickel I made went into this until it was obvious I could make a hell of a lot of money by merely dying. I became obsessed with this idea. I talked to a scientist I knew about life insurance (you should have some scientists among your friends—they think straight); this guy (his name is Dr. John Fisher) was a well-known metallurgist (and his wife's name is Josephine). I said, "John, how much life insurance have you got?" He said, "None." And I said, "What, you don't have *any* insurance?" and he said, "Hell no, what do I care what happens to Jo after I'm dead? I won't feel anything." It was release. I let my policy lapse.

On envy, well, I was nearly consumed with it, like being shot full of sulfuric acid. I have beaten it pretty well. I was put to the test recently when a young man dropped by (young people *do* seem to like me a lot) in a Lincoln Continental, and he was nineteen years old and had kept a diary of the Columbia riots which he had sold along with the movie rights. He said, "So far, I've made $27,000 from the riots." And I took it beautifully; I said, "Isn't that nice."

I'm richer now than I used to be. I'm a lot happier, too.

CASEY: What about your novel *Slaughterhouse-Five?*

VONNEGUT: It's . . . it's very thin . . . about as long as *The Bobbsey Twins*. This length has been considered a fault. *Ramparts* (*Ramparts* serialized the novel) called to ask if they had received all the manuscript. I said, "Yeah, that's it." I'm satisfied. They're satisfied. They just wanted to make sure they had all the paper they were entitled to.

But I think this is what a novel should be right now. I'd like, for example, to write books that *men* can read. I know that men don't read, and that bothers me. I would like to be a member of my community, and men in our society do not customarily value the services of a writer. To get their attention I should write short novels.

The reason novels were so thick for so long was that people had so much time to kill. I do not furnish transportation for my characters; I do not move them from one room to another; I do not send them up the stairs; they do not get dressed in the mornings; they do not put the ignition key in the lock, and turn on the engine, and let it warm up and look at all the gauges, and put the car in reverse, and back out, and drive to the filling station, and ask the guy there about the weather. You can fill up a good-size book with this connective tissue. People would be satisfied, too. I've often thought of taking one of my thin books (because people won't pay much for one) and adding a sash weight to it just to give someone the bulk he needs to pay seven or eight dollars for the thing, which is what I need to really eat and stuff.

There's the *Valley of the Dolls* solution, which is the Bernard Geis solution, which is to print the book on ¾-inch plywood, each page, and to print the type in the width of a newspaper column down the middle of the plywood. Then you've got a good-size book. But there're no words in it. Incidently, nobody's really complained yet.

CASEY: What about your novel *Slaughterhouse-Five*?

VONNEGUT: It was written to treat a disaster. I was present in the greatest massacre in European history, which was the destruction of Dresden by fire-bombing. So I said, "Okay, you were there."

The American and British air forces together killed 135,000 people in two hours. This is a world's record. It's never been done faster, not in the battle of Britain or Hiroshima. (In order to qualify as a massacre you have to kill *real* fast). But I was there, and there was no news about it in the American papers, it was so embarrassing. I was there—so say something about it.

The way we survived—we were in the stockyards in the middle of Dresden. How does a firestorm work? Waves and waves of planes come over carrying high explosives which open roofs, make lots of kindling, and drive the firemen underground. Then they take hundreds of thousands of little incendiary bombs (the size had been reduced from a foot and a half to the size of a shotgun shell by the end of the war) and scatter them. Then more high explosives until all the little fires join up into one apocalyptic flame with tornadoes around the edges sucking more and more, feeding the inferno.

Dresden was a highly ornamented city, like Paris. There were no air-raid shelters, just ordinary cellars, because a raid was not expected and the war was almost over.

We got through it, the Americans there, because we were quartered in the stockyards where it was wide and open and there was a meat locker three stories beneath the surface, the only decent shelter in the city. So we went down into the meat locker, and when we came up again the city was gone and everybody was dead. We walked for miles before we saw anybody else: all organic things were consumed.

Anyway, I came home in 1945, started writing about it, and

wrote about it, and *wrote about it*, and WROTE ABOUT IT. This thin book is about what it's like to write a book about a thing like that. I couldn't get much closer. I would head myself into my memory of it, the circuit breakers would kick out; I'd head in again, I'd back off. The book is a process of twenty years of this sort of living with Dresden and the aftermath. It's like Heinrich Böll's book, *Absent Without Leave*—stories about German soldiers with the war part missing. You see them leave and return, but there's this terrible hole in the middle. That is like my memory of Dresden; actually there's nothing there. It's a strange book. I'm pleased with it.

BELLAMY: In *Slaughterhouse-Five* you talk about the form of the Tralfamadorian novel—a group of moments all seen simultaneously. Do you think any contemporary experimenters may be approaching this in their own works right now—writers such as Donald Barthelme, Ronald Sukenick, Rudolph Wurlitzer, or maybe even you yourself?

VONNEGUT: Well, I suppose we're all trying to. One thing we used to talk about—when I was out in Iowa—was that the limiting factor is the reader. No other art requires the audience to be a performer. You have to count on the reader's being a good performer, and you may write music which he absolutely can't perform—in which case it's a bust. Those writers you mentioned and myself are teaching an audience how to play this kind of music in their heads. It's a learning process, and *The New Yorker* has been a very good institution of the sort needed. They have a captive audience, and they come out every week, and people finally catch on to Barthelme, for instance, and are able to perform that sort of thing in their heads and enjoy it. I think the same is true of S. J. Perelman; I do not think that Perelman would be appreciated if suddenly his collected works were to be published now to be seen for the first time. It would be gibberish. A learning process is required to appreciate Perelman, although it's very easy to do once you learn how to do it. Yeah, I think the readers are coming along; that's a problem; I think writers have tried to do it always and have failed because there's been no audience for what they've done; nobody's performed their music.

BELLAMY: You've mentioned before that Donald Barthelme is one of your favorite writers. . . .

VONNEGUT: Well, he's a friend of mine now. We've gotten to be very friendly. There was a meeting of PEN—International PEN in Stockholm—and people from all over the world were invited, and the two invited representatives of the United States were Donald Barthelme and myself—and we're both sons of architects.

BELLAMY: Do you have any other favorites—younger writers? I was thinking especially of innovative writers like Barthelme.

VONNEGUT: I'm not really partial to radicals. I like a lot of stuff. I think there's a golden age of literature, extraordinarily good work being done. And there's nobody to read it all.

BELLAMY: How would you characterize the new kind of fiction being written now? You've mentioned that you think readers are becoming better trained. Do you think writers are doing anything in particular that you could identify?

VONNEGUT: Writers have had to change because the audience changes. People writing for the theatre have discovered that audiences can no longer stand exposition. They used to be able to. We have a much shorter attention span perhaps, because of television and the film. We've been educated to quick cuts and very little exposition, and if you revive a play like *You Can't Take It With You* or *Ah, Wilderness!* or any of those things which were successes in very recent times, the audience becomes very itchy. You just get the feeling all around you that people are saying, "Got it, got it, got it." You know, get on with it, come on, come on. And let's get moving. It used to be a playwright's responsibility to tell the audience who these people were and what they hoped for and all that, and the audience required that—and they can't stand that anymore, and there are other changes. I think Watergate is going to have an enormous effect on what is being read. Number one on the best-seller list is me, and number two is Wicker, and I think there's a political decision on the part of the readers. I think they are deciding to go around and see what there is on the lunatic fringe.

BELLAMY: One of the techniques that a lot of writers have been using—and you do it in *Breakfast of Champions*—is to put yourself in the book as yourself, as the self-conscious creator of the whole show. Do you think this is a more honest way of approaching fiction? How did you come to do it yourself in *Breakfast*? Of course you did it in *Slaughterhouse-Five*, too.

VONNEGUT: An inner urgency. I don't know. You probably get to a point where you can afford to do more self-indulgent things. I am at the point now . . . my publishers tell me I'm at the point where absolutely anything I write is going to sell extremely well, that it's going to sell phenomenally. That's not a dream—it's true.

BELLAMY: There's a curious thing; a rare book dealer sent a Xerox of your manuscript of *Breakfast of Champions* to a friend of mine. Apparently it was sent to a few reviewers. And it had a different ending! It had you in an asylum with Dwayne Hoover. You mentioned that you always knew you'd write yourself into a loony bin and now you had to figure out how to write yourself out. Apparently you did by the time the galleys got out. Can you tell me about that?

VONNEGUT: Well, the way the Xeroxes got in the hands of people . . . if you're well-known, there's going to be a minor industry operating in your publishing house without anybody knowing it. Which is that somebody is going to be offered some money for a Xerox of a script which hasn't been shown to anybody yet.

BELLAMY: Oh, so that was not licit. . . .

VONNEGUT: Whatever that rare book dealer's got is a black-market item.

BELLAMY: Oh boy, I didn't know that. . . .

VONNEGUT: I mean, it's all right with me, I don't care. . . . And movie companies will pay for Xeroxes; whoever sells them has no right to them; it will be some secretary or editor or just anybody. That's how *Slaughterhouse-Five* was sold to the movies. A guy bought it on the basis of a bootleg Xerox.

BELLAMY: What about this different ending to *Breakfast*—at what point did you change that?

VONNEGUT: Well, I was working on it and working on it and working on it and finally said all right that's *it*, and . . . that's the bootleg copy you saw. And there was a lot of messenger work, as these days I live about six blocks from my publisher. So I'd send them pieces of manuscript, and they'd send proof back and forth, hand-carried by people. And a couple of young people in the production department—I'm sorry I don't know their names—showed up with some part of the script, I forget what, and one of them said, "I didn't like the ending." And I said, "What's the matter with it?" And they said, "We don't like it; that's not the way we think it should end; we just thought we should say so." And I said, "Okay, I'll think about it," and thanked them. And I should know their names because—they were right!

CASEY: One last question. . . .

VONNEGUT: I'll give you a disturbing answer. People are programmed, just like computers with this tape feeding out. When I was teaching student writers, I suddenly realized in most cases what I was doing was reaching into the mouth, taking hold of the piece of tape, pulling gently to see if I could read what was printed on it.

There is this thing called the university, and everybody goes there now. And there are these things called teachers who make students read this book with good ideas or that book with good ideas until that's where we get our ideas. We don't think them; we read them in books.

I like Utopian talk, speculation about what our planet should be, anger about what our planet is.

I think writers are the most important members of society, not just potentially but actually. Good writers must have and stand by their own ideas.

I like everything there is about being a writer except the way my neighbors treat me. Because I honor them for what they are, and they really do find me irrelevant on Cape Cod. There's my state representative. I campaigned for him, and he got drunk one night and came over and said, "You know, I can't understand a word you write and neither can any of your neighbors . . . so why don't you change your style, so why not write something people will like?" He was just telling me for my own good. He was a former English major at Brown.

CASEY: Did he win?

VONNEGUT: He went crazy. He really went bughouse, finally.

The Interviewers

JOE DAVID BELLAMY has published fiction, poetry, articles, reviews, and interviews in *The Atlantic Monthly*, *Partisan Review*, *New American Review*, *Iowa Review*, *Chicago Review*, Klinkowitz's and Somer's *The Vonnegut Statement*, and elsewhere. His *Apocalypse: Dominant Contemporary Forms* (1972) is a major college writing text published by the J. B. Lippincott Company. Educated at Duke University, Antioch College, and the Iowa Writers Workshop, Bellamy teaches writing and literature at Saint Lawrence University in Canton, New York.

JOHN CASEY is a writer, a lawyer, and a reviewer for such magazines as the *New York Times Book Review*. His fiction has appeared in *The New Yorker*, *Sports Illustrated*, and *Redbook*.

PAT ENSWORTH is Chicago editor of *Fiction*, the tabloid edited by Mark Mirsky and Donald Barthelme. She recently received the J. Scott Clark Award for creative writing at Northwestern University, where she is a student.

JEROME KLINKOWITZ's essays and reviews have appeared in *Modern Fiction Studies*, *North American Review*, *Book World*,

Chicago Review, fiction international, The Village Voice, and elsewhere. His recent books, with John Somer, are *Innovative Fiction* (Dell, 1972) and *The Vonnegut Statement* (Delacorte/Seymour Lawrence and Delta Books, 1973). He holds degrees from Marquette University and the University of Wisconsin and teaches at the University of Northern Iowa. His work in progress, *Literary Disruptions: The Making of a Post-Contemporary American Fiction,* will be published by the University of Illinois Press.

CAROLE SPEARIN McCAULEY's work (articles, poetry, satire, fiction, reviews) has appeared in more than forty magazines and anthologies in this country and Germany. She has recently completed an experimental novel, *Happenthing in Travel On,* sections of which have been published in anthologies from Ballantine Books and from Something Else Press, and she is completing a book on computers and creativity for Praeger.

JOHN O'BRIEN is author of *Interviews with Black Writers* (1973), published by Liveright, and editor of a forthcoming story anthology, *No Signs from Heaven* (Dell). His work has appeared in *The American Scholar, Studies in Black Literature,* and *fiction international.* He teaches literature at Aurora College.

ROBERT SCHOLES is Professor of English at Brown University and, through the *New York Times Book Review* and his seminal book *The Fabulators* (Oxford, 1967), one of the major commentators upon the work of John Hawkes, John Barth, and Kurt Vonnegut, Jr. Others of his books are *The Nature of Narrative* (with Robert Kellogg, Oxford, 1966), and *Approaches to the Novel: Materials for a Poetics* (Chandler, 1961). He is now finishing a book of critical pieces to be called *The Illiberal Imagination.*